D1784197

FRONTPAGE® 2000
FOR
DUMMIES®

Quick Reference

by Damon Dean

IDG
BOOKS
WORLDWIDE

IDG Books Worldwide, Inc.
An International Data Group Compan

Foster City, CA ✦ Chicago, IL ✦ Indianapolis, IN ✦ Ne

FrontPage® 2000 For Dummies® Quick Reference

Published by
IDG Books Worldwide, Inc.
An International Data Group Company
919 E. Hillsdale Blvd.
Suite 400
Foster City, CA 94404
www.idgbooks.com (IDG Books Worldwide Web site)
www.dummies.com (Dummies Press Web site)

Library of Congress Catalog Card No.: 99-60742

ISBN: 0-7645-0499-1

Printed in the United States of America

10 9 8 7 6 5 4 3 2 1

1P/RX/QT/ZZ/IN

Distributed in the United States by IDG Books Worldwide, Inc.

Distributed by CDG Books Canada Inc. for Canada; by Transworld Publishers Limited in the United Kingdom; by IDG Norge Books for Norway; by IDG Sweden Books for Sweden; by Woodslane Pty. Ltd. for Australia; by Woodslane (NZ) Ltd. for New Zealand; by TransQuest Publishers Pte Ltd. for Singapore, Malaysia, Thailand, Indonesia, and Hong Kong; by ICG Muse, Inc. for Japan; by Norma Comunicaciones S.A. for Colombia; by Intersoft for South Africa; by Le Monde en Tique for France; by International Thomson Publishing for Germany, Austria and Switzerland; by Distribuidora Cuspide for Argentina; by Livraria Cultura for Brazil; by Ediciones ZETA S.C.R. Ltda. for Peru; by WS Computer Publishing Corporation, Inc., for the Philippines; by Contemporanea de Ediciones for Venezuela; by Express Computer Distributors for the Caribbean and West Indies; by Micronesia Media Distributor, Inc. for Micronesia; by Grupo Editorial Norma S.A. for Guatemala; by Chips Computadoras S.A. de C.V. for Mexico; by Editorial Norma de Panama S.A. for Panama; by American Bookshops for Finland. Authorized Sales Agent: Anthony Rudkin Associates for the Middle East and North Africa.

For general information on IDG Books Worldwide's books in the U.S., please call our Consumer Customer Service department at 800-762-2974. For reseller information, including discounts and premium sales, please call our Reseller Customer Service department at 800-434-3422.

For information on where to purchase IDG Books Worldwide's books outside the U.S., please contact our International Sales department at 317-596-5530 or fax 317-596-5692.

For consumer information on foreign language translations, please contact our Customer Service department at 1-800-434-3422, fax 317-596-5692, or e-mail rights@idgbooks.com.

For information on licensing foreign or domestic rights, please phone +1-650-655-3109.

For sales inquiries and special prices for bulk quantities, please contact our Sales department at 650-655-3200 or write to the address above.

For information on using IDG Books Worldwide's books in the classroom or for ordering examination copies, please contact our Educational Sales department at 800-434-2086 or fax 317-596-5499.

For press review copies, author interviews, or other publicity information, please contact our Public Relations department at 650-655-3000 or fax 650-655-3299.

For authorization to photocopy items for corporate, personal, or educational use, please contact Copyright Clearance Center, 222 Rosewood Drive, Danvers, MA 01923, or fax 978-750-4470.

About the Author

Damon Dean is the author of *Web Channel Development For Dummies,* also published by IDG Books Worldwide, Inc., as well as *The Pocket Tour of Multimedia on the Internet,* published by Sybex. The author of nearly 100 articles on computers and gaming, Dean also claims to know a thing or two about the Internet. After spending six delirious years in the multimedia and computer games industry, he now spends his time "Working the Web™" for 415 Productions. As is required of all UCLA graduates, Dean is currently finishing up his first black-and-white movie short in his spare time.

ABOUT IDG BOOKS WORLDWIDE

Welcome to the world of IDG Books Worldwide.

IDG Books Worldwide, Inc., is a subsidiary of International Data Group, the world's largest publisher of computer-related information and the leading global provider of information services on information technology. IDG was founded more than 30 years ago by Patrick J. McGovern and now employs more than 9,000 people worldwide. IDG publishes more than 290 computer publications in over 75 countries. More than 90 million people read one or more IDG publications each month.

Launched in 1990, IDG Books Worldwide is today the #1 publisher of best-selling computer books in the United States. We are proud to have received eight awards from the Computer Press Association in recognition of editorial excellence and three from Computer Currents' First Annual Readers' Choice Awards. Our best-selling ...For Dummies® series has more than 50 million copies in print with translations in 31 languages. IDG Books Worldwide, through a joint venture with IDG's Hi-Tech Beijing, became the first U.S. publisher to publish a computer book in the People's Republic of China. In record time, IDG Books Worldwide has become the first choice for millions of readers around the world who want to learn how to better manage their businesses.

Our mission is simple: Every one of our books is designed to bring extra value and skill-building instructions to the reader. Our books are written by experts who understand and care about our readers. The knowledge base of our editorial staff comes from years of experience in publishing, education, and journalism — experience we use to produce books to carry us into the new millennium. In short, we care about books, so we attract the best people. We devote special attention to details such as audience, interior design, use of icons, and illustrations. And because we use an efficient process of authoring, editing, and desktop publishing our books electronically, we can spend more time ensuring superior content and less time on the technicalities of making books.

You can count on our commitment to deliver high-quality books at competitive prices on topics you want to read about. At IDG Books Worldwide, we continue in the IDG tradition of delivering quality for more than 30 years. You'll find no better book on a subject than one from IDG Books Worldwide.

John Kilcullen
Chairman and CEO
IDG Books Worldwide, Inc.

Steven Berkowitz
President and Publisher
IDG Books Worldwide, Inc.

WINNER

Eighth Annual
Computer Press
Awards ≥1992

WINNER

Ninth Annual
Computer Press
Awards ≥1993

WINNER

Tenth Annual
Computer Press
Awards ≥1994

WINNER

Eleventh Annual
Computer Press
Awards ≥1995

IDG is the world's leading IT media, research and exposition company. Founded in 1964, IDG had 1997 revenues of $2.05 billion and has more than 9,000 employees worldwide. IDG offers the widest range of media options that reach IT buyers in 75 countries representing 95% of worldwide IT spending. IDG's diverse product and services portfolio spans six key areas including print publishing, online publishing, expositions and conferences, market research, education and training, and global marketing services. More than 90 million people read one or more of IDG's 290 magazines and newspapers, including IDG's leading global brands — Computerworld, PC World, Network World, Macworld and the Channel World family of publications. IDG Books Worldwide is one of the fastest-growing computer book publishers in the world, with more than 700 titles in 36 languages. The "...For Dummies®" series alone has more than 50 million copies in print. IDG offers online users the largest network of technology-specific Web sites around the world through IDG.net (http://www.idg.net), which comprises more than 225 targeted Web sites in 55 countries worldwide. International Data Corporation (IDC) is the world's largest provider of information technology data, analysis and consulting, with research centers in over 41 countries and more than 400 research analysts worldwide. IDG World Expo is a leading producer of more than 168 globally branded conferences and expositions in 35 countries including E3 (Electronic Entertainment Expo), Macworld Expo, ComNet, Windows World Expo, ICE (Internet Commerce Expo), Agenda, DEMO, and Spotlight. IDG's training subsidiary, ExecuTrain, is the world's largest computer training company, with more than 230 locations worldwide and 785 training courses. IDG Marketing Services helps industry-leading IT companies build international brand recognition by developing global integrated marketing programs via IDG's print, online and exposition products worldwide. Further information about the company can be found at www.idg.com.   1/24/99

Dedication

For Tom and Nancy. For everything . . .

Author's Acknowledgments

There's nothing like an insane deadline to bring out the best in people. When IDG Books approached me to write this book in . . . GULP . . . five weeks, I wasn't sure that I was up to the challenge. Once it was all said and done, however, two things were clear. One, I spent more time up at 3:00 in the morning typing than I did through my four years of college. And two, the team at IDG Books proved once again that they are the best at their craft: making books that help people learn.

It's with that in mind that I want to thank first Steve Hayes for giving me another shot at making my deadlines. The editorial team, headed by Pam Mourouzis and including Bill Barton, Billie Williams, and Diane Smith, was solid from start to finish, and I sincerely appreciate the patience they demonstrated in converting my garbled ramblings into a cohesive, streamlined reference guide.

Closer to home, I'd like to thank my family and friends for keeping me going and not-so-subtly reminding me that I did have a life to be found on the far side of this journey. In particular, I want to give a shout out to Grace Stanat and Jeff Southard, the principals of 415 Productions, where I work. They didn't gripe even one little bit when I decided to write this book a mere two weeks after I started work. Quite to the contrary, they were supportive all the way. I'd also like to thank Scott Zucca, whose valuable help in setting up a FrontPage 2000 server here at 415 proved that nearly everything I thought about FrontPage servers was wrong.

Publisher's Acknowledgments

We're proud of this book; please register your comments through our IDG Books Worldwide Online Registration Form located at: http://my2cents.dummies.com.

Some of the people who helped bring this book to market include the following:

Acquisitions, Editorial, and Media Development

Senior Project Editor: Pamela Mourouzis

Associate Acquisitions Editor: Steven H. Hayes

Copy Editors: William A. Barton, Billie A. Williams

Technical Editor: Lee Musick

Editorial Manager: Rev Mengle

Editorial Assistant: Alison Walthall

Production

Project Coordinator: Tom Missler

Layout and Graphics: Linda Boyer, J. Tyler Connor, Maridee Ennis, Angela F. Hunckler, Drew Moore, Brent Savage, Janet Seib, Brian Torwelle

Proofreaders: Kelli Botta, Chris Collins, Nancy Price, Rebecca Senninger, Ethel M. Winslow, Janet M. Withers

Indexer: Ty Koontz

Special Help

Leah Cameron, Susan Diane Smith

General and Administrative

IDG Books Worldwide, Inc.: John Kilcullen, CEO; Steven Berkowitz, President and Publisher

IDG Books Technology Publishing: Brenda McLaughlin, Senior Vice President and Group Publisher

Dummies Technology Press and Dummies Editorial: Diane Graves Steele, Vice President and Associate Publisher; Mary Bednarek, Director of Acquisitions and Product Development; Kristin A. Cocks, Editorial Director

Dummies Trade Press: Kathleen A. Welton, Vice President and Publisher; Kevin Thornton, Acquisitions Manager

IDG Books Production for Dummies Press: Michael R. Britton, Vice President of Production and Creative Services; Cindy L. Phipps, Manager of Project Coordination, Production Proofreading, and Indexing; Kathie S. Schutte, Supervisor of Page Layout; Shelley Lea, Supervisor of Graphics and Design; Debbie J. Gates, Production Systems Specialist; Robert Springer, Supervisor of Proofreading; Debbie Stailey, Special Projects Coordinator; Tony Augsburger, Supervisor of Reprints and Bluelines

Dummies Packaging and Book Design: Patty Page, Manager, Promotions Marketing

◆

The publisher would like to give special thanks to Patrick J. McGovern, without whom this book would not have been possible.

◆

Contents at a Glance

Table of Contents

How to Use This Book

Work the Web. That's the new marketing catch phrase for "Spend a lot of time trying to figure out how to put stuff on the Internet and then get really frustrated after a few hours because you have nothing to show for all your work." No, thanks — I'll pass. I'd rather log on, do what I need to get done, and move on to something else . . . like watching *ER* on TV, for example.

If getting things done quickly and efficiently is your style, you're in luck. *FrontPage 2000 For Dummies Quick Reference* isn't for tech-heads or diehard computer geeks. It's for people who want to publish Web pages by using FrontPage 2000 and who may need a no-nonsense, easy-to-use guide to point them in the right direction from time to time.

You have questions, I have answers . . . and now, so do you.

This Book: Who Needs It?

FrontPage is one of the most popular tools for developing Web pages on the Internet. And now that FrontPage 2000 is part of the Microsoft Office suite, look out! Hundreds of thousands of people are going to fire up this program and utter a collective "Huh?" as they try to figure out what FrontPage 2000 can do.

Most people don't have the time — or the inclination, for that matter — to wade through the too-technical software user guides, the jargony "hands-on" articles, or the dreaded online FAQ (Frequently Asked Questions) lists. When I have a question about software, I want a simple answer in plain English, in a convenient place where I can get to it easily. And I bet you're the same way.

FrontPage 2000 is a big program, with lots of new features for Web developers big and small. You may never use, need, or want most of those features, but I guarantee that, every now and then, you'll come across a question that stumps you or (even worse) escapes your memory. That's when this book is going to become your best friend, with quick, easy-to-read answers in plain English.

As with most software programs, the more you work with FrontPage 2000, the more interesting, frustrating, and powerful it seems. FrontPage works as easily as a bare-bones HTML editor as it does as a massive Web publishing system. Within the pages of this book, I show you tips and tricks for creating and publishing great Web pages in FrontPage. Then again, if you just forgot the location of the Print button, I can point you in that direction, too.

FrontPage 2000 can be as simple or as complex as you choose to make it. My goal is to get you (ugh, I can't believe what I'm about to say) where you want to go with this new Office 2000 program, if for no other reason than to make your work life a little easier and perhaps help you to impress a colleague or two.

Parts, Parts, and More Parts

You may notice as you peruse the Table of Contents that I split this book up into several parts revolving largely around the tasks that you want to achieve by using FrontPage. Each part covers either a major functional component of the program (such as the HTML editor) or a really big application of the program (such as building a Web page).

Here's how I divided up the book:

✦ **Part I: Getting to Know FrontPage 2000.** Get ready for a brief rundown of everything you ever wanted to know about FrontPage 2000! Part I familiarizes you with FrontPage's setup and explains what's new in FrontPage 2000. I hope that this part helps you get your head around this powerful program.

✦ **Part II: The Basics of Webs and Web Pages.** Want to get up and running in a hurry? Then Part II is for you! Pick up the basics of creating a Web page in FrontPage 2000 right here. This part also introduces you to some of the program's more common tasks.

✦ **Part III: Working with FrontPage 2000 Projects.** Building a Web site entails more than just creating one page. From using templates and themes to organizing Web content and publishing it to the Internet, FrontPage 2000 offers a host of tools to assist you in maintaining and improving your Web site. Part III shows you how to put all these features in FrontPage 2000 to good use.

✦ **Part IV: Building Web Sites with the FrontPage Editor.** FrontPage 2000 offers one of the best (and most advanced) Web page editors on the market. If you want to build cool Web pages by using this editor, check out this part.

✦ **Part V: Image Editing in FrontPage 2000.** As do other Microsoft Office products, FrontPage 2000 includes several image-editing options. Part V shows you how to manipulate your images in ways you probably never thought possible!

✦ **Part VI: Using FrontPage 2000 with Office 2000.** Want to know how FrontPage 2000 works with its Office 2000 brethren? This part makes everything clear, showing you such neat tricks as how to embed Excel spreadsheets in a Web page.

✦ **Part VII: Advanced Features in FrontPage 2000.** Ready for the big time — JavaScript, Java, Dynamic HTML? In Part VII, you can find out how FrontPage 2000 supports the more advanced Internet technologies and how the program can help you integrate these cool new technologies into your site.

Within each part of this book, I organize the main topics not by function or by difficulty, but rather alphabetically (except in Part I — there, topics are organized chronologically to get you up and running in FrontPage as quickly as possible). That makes topics easier to find when you're desperately searching for a particular piece of information. All the topics in this book are short, sweet, and to the point; if a topic has subsections, those subsections are even shorter, sweeter, and more to the point. That's the idea of this book: Find it, get your answer, and move along little doggie.

How to Use This Book

You can use this book in lots of ways. Here are a few tried-and-true suggestions:

✦ **Check the Table of Contents.** I labored for weeks to polish that thing. Most of this book's major topics and concepts appear in the Table of Contents, organized alphabetically. That's the best place to start if you have a question about something in the program.

✦ **Head to the index.** IDG Books spent some cold, hard cash hiring people to review this book and Index to make sure that FrontPage 2000's important points appear throughout both. If you have a question about a concept or specific function that isn't immediately apparent in the Table of Contents, jump to the back of the book and check out the Index.

✦ **Browse the dictionary.** No, not Webster's. At the end of this book, I include a Glossary (okay, so it's not actually a *dictionary*) containing a number of the key concepts and definitions that I use liberally throughout the book. These definitions may provide the spark that lights your way toward the answer to whatever question you have.

✦ **Laugh. Cry. Read.** You could read this entire book during lunch if you *really* wanted to, but I didn't try to work any secret plot lines, devilishly good-looking characters, or romance into this book, so doing so probably isn't worth your time. (That said, I do think that some of the one-liners are pretty good.) Instead, peruse the sections that interest you, and then use the book to answer specific questions as they arise.

Conventions Used in This Book

This is a how-to book, so it shouldn't come as much of a surprise to you to find a number of commands littered throughout the book.

If you come across a command such as

Ctrl+Z

run away as fast as you can! No, seriously, this simply means that you should hold down the the Ctrl key and then press the Z key. No need to type the plus sign, as it won't do much good and will no doubt only get you mad at me.

You'll also see quite a few commands like this in the book:

File⇨Open

When you see this kind of command, you're going to want to use the mouse or keyboard to perform an action with one of FrontPage's menus. The underlined letters are the keyboard *hot keys* for the command. You can use the hot keys by pressing the Alt key. To use the keyboard in the preceding example, you'd first press the Alt key, then the F key to active the File menu, and finally the O key to initiate the Open command.

There's a pretty good chance that I'll tell you to type something. When that happens, you'll see the text that you're to type in boldface, like this:

Type **b:setup** in the Run dialog box.

In these cases, make sure to type the text just as you see it on the page.

Finally, Internet addresses will appear in this font.

Icon Mania

I have no idea who invented icons in computer books, but that person is a bona fide genius. Not only do icons take up space, but the little critters are also a nice and easy way of telling you, the reader, "Hey, you, reader — look here! I've got something I *really* want you to see!"

And what do the icons in this book mean, you ask? Here's the deal:

This icon is the been-there-done-that marker. I've been there, and I know an easier way. Follow my lead, and I'll show you the way home!

"Watch out for that tree!" If you see this icon, know that it signals a potential pitfall that can cause you a lot of grief.

 In the beginning was FrontPage. Then FrontPage 98 appeared on the Web publishing horizon. And now comes — ta-daaa — FrontPage 2000. Although you can use this book as a reference for all the versions of FrontPage, know that, whenever you see this icon, you're reading about something that's new to FrontPage 2000.

 If you really need more information, this icon points you to additional resources.

So You Want to Know More Before You Even Get Started?

That's fair. I always like to read the last page of a novel before I read the rest of it. If you can't find the information that you need in this book, here are a few other places to look:

✦ www.microsoft.com: That news shouldn't be much of a shocker. From the Microsoft home page, you can get to the Office Web site, where you can get all the latest information about FrontPage 2000.

✦ www.builder.com: At this site, you can find out the latest on how other Web creators are using FrontPage 2000.

✦ www.idg.net: Want the latest news on FrontPage 2000 and a host of other Internet-related products? Then this is the Web site for you.

Getting to Know FrontPage 2000

FrontPage 2000 is one of the most powerful — and popular — Web publishing tools ever created. In no time at all, you're going to be creating all sorts of really cool stuff for the Web.

Still a little wary about how this program works and what it can do? Don't worry. This part provides a basic overview of what FrontPage is, how it works, and where it fits into the Microsoft Office 2000 family of products.

In this part . . .

✓ **Understanding what FrontPage does**

✓ **Finding out what's new in FrontPage 2000**

✓ **Understanding how FrontPage 2000 is integrated into Office 2000**

✓ **Touring FrontPage 2000 and the other programs within it**

What Is FrontPage 2000, and What Can I Do with It?

FrontPage 2000 is what Microsoft calls a "Web publishing solution." Sounds complicated, doesn't it? In reality, "Web publishing solution" is just a fancy term for making Web pages and putting them on the Internet. Of course, "making Web pages and putting them on the Internet" doesn't sound nearly as sexy and, therefore, wouldn't sell as well.

FrontPage 2000 is an all-in-one Web publishing tool that's made for big-time Web publishing companies (such as Yahoo! and ESPN), small companies, and personal users. By *all-in-one,* I mean that you cannot only create individual Web pages but also use FrontPage 2000 to publish Web pages to the Internet, generate tracking reports about those Web pages, and effectively administer an entire Web site once it's on the Net . . . all from within the same program.

Of course, you may never want to administer an entire Web site and use all that functionality, and that's okay. If you just want to use FrontPage to build plain old HTML pages on your own and put them up on the Internet the way you've always done, that's fine. FrontPage is exceptionally flexible and scalable; it can grow with you as your Web site needs grow.

The following is a quick rundown of the kinds of things you can do in FrontPage 2000:

✦ **Use it as an HTML editor.** You can pound out as much HTML as you like, but in FrontPage, why would you want to? You can lay out a page visually by using graphics, text, and even Java applets and have FrontPage generate all the HTML for you!

Embedding Java applets in Web pages can be tricky business. *See* Part VII to find out how it's done in FrontPage 2000.

✦ **Use it as a Web site builder.** Not only can you create Web pages in FrontPage, but you can also view the layout of your entire Web site, automatically change links to Web pages, and organize pages and folders by using the familiar Windows drag-and-drop function.

✦ **Use it as an image editor.** Although FrontPage 2000 doesn't have the most powerful image editor, it does have some handy image-editing features built right in. For example, you can rotate and flip images and vary their brightness and contrast.

+ **Use it as a Web site publisher.** Tired of having to use an editor to build your Web pages, find the appropriate FTP program, and then remember which are the new files that you want to post to your Web site? By using FrontPage, you can control how your Web site content looks and how and when that content gets sent to the Internet.

+ **Use it as a Web site manager.** You can run reports on your Web site and get vital information about the status of broken hyperlinks, Web pages currently under construction, and even which pages will load the slowest.

+ **Use it as a source control manager.** *Source control* is a software term that describes the management of files — in this case, HTML pages, graphics, JavaScript, and any other files within your Web site — across multiple users. By managing source control, you can determine who works on a file, when that person works on it, and what privileges the person has while working on it.

Although anyone working on a site can use source control, it's usually the Web site administrator who sets permissions for other users and tracks who has which files checked into and out of the source control manager. In FrontPage 2000, unlike previous versions of FrontPage, source control is built into the product itself.

Whew! That's a lot of functionality for one software program!

What's New in FrontPage 2000?

If you own a copy of FrontPage 98, many of the points I mentioned in the preceding section should seem familiar. FrontPage 2000, however, is a complete overhaul of previous versions of FrontPage and represents the largest upgrade of any of the Office 2000 software products.

The addition of FrontPage 2000 to Microsoft Office 2000 marks the largest change to the product. FrontPage 2000 now shares links to those products through the Microsoft OLE and ActiveX controls and an interface that's similar to other Office products. In noncomputer speak, that means that you can do things that were previously impossible, such as embedding an "editable" Excel spreadsheet into a Web page.

OLE and ActiveX are two Microsoft technologies that are embedded within Office and Windows, respectively. OLE is an interchange format that enables the different Office programs to share a common language among them. In contrast, ActiveX is a series of

Windows interface commands that enable Web builders to call general Windows applications such as the Media Player, or even another application, and embed them within a Web page.

 In addition to its integration with the other Office products, FrontPage 2000 finally got a little integration of its own. In FrontPage 98, one of the more annoying features was having the FrontPage Explorer (for managing the site) and the FrontPage Editor (for building pages) as separate applications. Not anymore! In FrontPage 2000, these applications are melded into one program.

 Site management is the other major feature upgrade in FrontPage 2000. Although previous versions of FrontPage enabled good site administration, the addition of source control and site reporting make FrontPage 2000 a better tool for companies that need to administer large sites with multiple content creators.

See Part III for more information about FrontPage's site administration features.

 In addition to the major changes, FrontPage 2000 features a number of smaller upgrades, including the following:

+ Pixel precise positioning of objects on Web pages

+ 100 percent preservation of HTML

+ Addition of the Microsoft Script Editor, a JavaScript and VB Script tool (***See*** Part VII.)

+ Automation of tasks, such as the updating of hyperlinks within a Web site

+ Browser-specific targeting for Web page content

+ New customizable Web site themes that can give a site a ton of different styles and looks

How FrontPage 2000 Is Organized

FrontPage 2000 contains a multitude of features, mini-applications, and menus, all wrapped up in one tidy little package. Still, maneuvering around FrontPage 2000 can baffle anyone. So to better orient you, I'm including the following screen shot of a typical FrontPage 2000 interface. You also see figure callouts for a number of features. Pay particular attention to the callouts, because you're no doubt going to find yourself using those features the most.

Formatting Toobar

Views bar

Standard Toobar

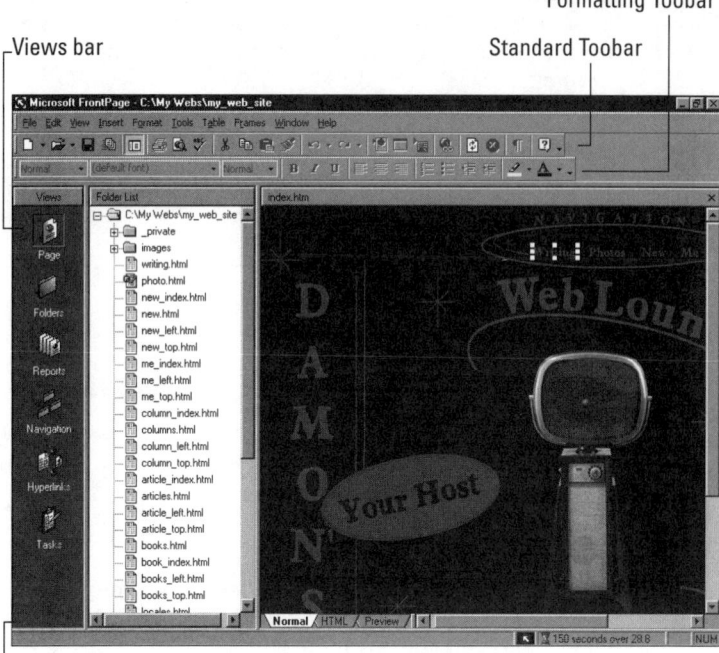

Picture Toolbar

Why Does FrontPage 2000 Look Like Microsoft Word?

If you looked at FrontPage 2000 and then turned your head away really quickly, you might think for a moment that you'd just seen a copy of Microsoft Word 2000. That's because FrontPage 2000 closely mimics Microsoft Word 2000, right down to the menus and toolbars.

Don't believe me? Check out the following two figures.

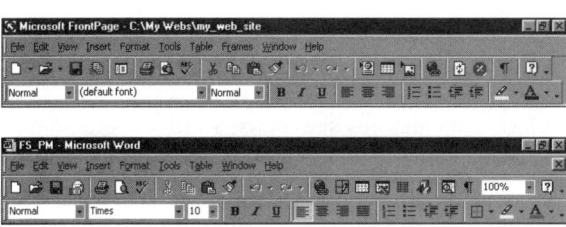

Microsoft's idea here is that providing a familiar and integrated approach to Office 2000's various product interfaces helps you, the Web builder, have an easier time getting a handle on using the products.

The Views Bar

It's pretty hard not to notice the Views Bar after you fire up FrontPage 2000 for the first time. The Views Bar's big menu, with all its icons running down the left-hand side of the screen, makes accessing the vast majority of features in FrontPage 2000 easy.

Each Views Bar icon represents a different feature in FrontPage 2000. To jump to a FrontPage feature, simply click the corresponding icon. The new feature appears in the right three-quarters of the screen, below the menus and toolbars.

If you don't like the Views Bar, you can turn it off by right-clicking the bar and choosing Hide Views Bar from the pop-up menu. Presto! The Views Bar disappears. After you turn off the Views Bar, you can still toggle your view within FrontPage by choosing one of the six views from the View menu. (The section "Viewing FrontPage from All Six Sides" explains the FrontPage views.)

If you want to change the size of the icons in the Views Bar, right-click the Views Bar and choose Small Icons from the pop-up menu.

Viewing FrontPage from All Six Sides

FrontPage 2000 features six key views to represent major components that you may or may not use, depending on your Web project. The following list describes these views:

    ✦ **Page View:** The Page View — known as the FrontPage Editor in previous versions of the product — is where you build all your Web pages. Within the Page View, you can review a Web page in three different ways. You select the Normal tab to use FrontPage's drag-and-drop visual HTML Editor. In addition, you can edit HTML directly through the HTML tab. You can also preview the pages in the Preview tab, which mimics the Internet Explorer Web browser.

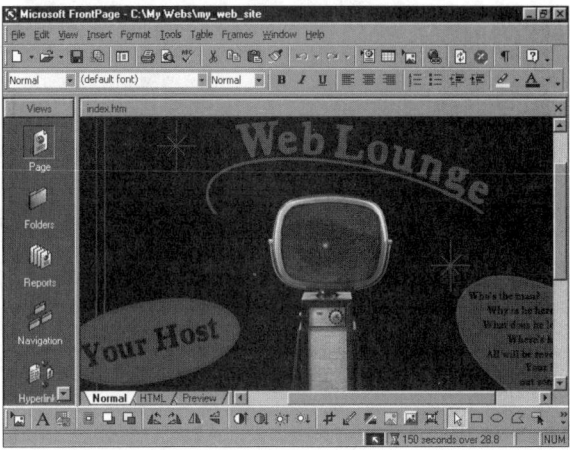

✦ **Folders View:** The Folders View is pretty much how it sounds. This view displays a typical Windows 98 Explorer menu, making all your Web project's files and folders easily accessible within FrontPage. From this view, you can also drag and drop files, which makes adding and deleting content easy.

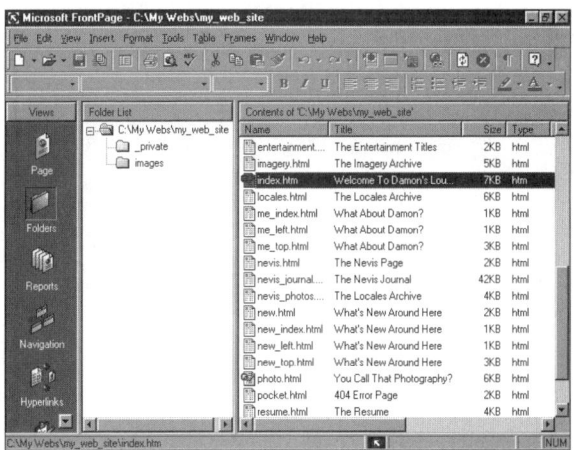

TIP

A Folder List also appears in the Folders View. You can access the Folder List in the other FrontPage views by choosing View⇨Folder List.

✦ **Reports View:** If you select the Reports View, you get an immediate Site Summary, which gives you a bird's-eye view of what's working (or not working, if, say, you have some broken hyperlinks!) within your Web site. From the Reports View, you can also run a more detailed series of reports that give you immediate information about the status of various aspects of your Web site, such as load times or hyperlink status.

See Part III for more information about all the various reports that FrontPage 2000 can generate for your Web site.

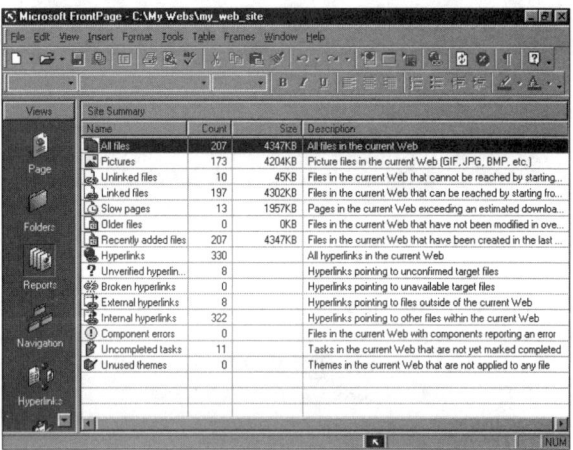

✦ **Navigation View:** The Navigation View provides a visual representation of all the pages on your Web site and the pages' hierarchical order. By dragging around the pages, you can change the relationships of those pages to one another and organize the pages of your site more effectively.

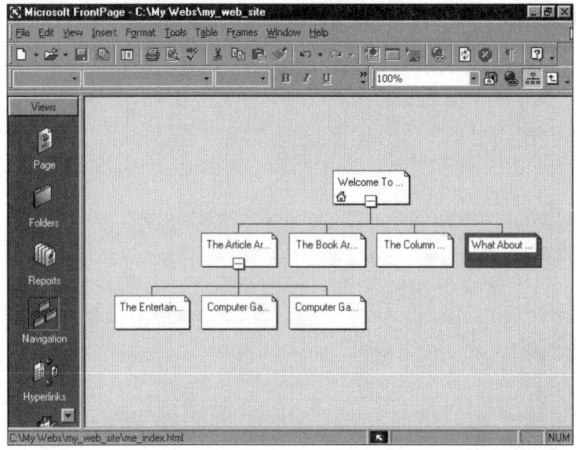

✦ **Hyperlinks View:** Figuring out how your Web pages connect to one another can be a serious chore. The Hyperlinks View gives you a graphical representation of how every Web page connects to every other page within your Web site, which can be particularly useful if you want to see how your pages are connected. In addition, the Hyperlinks View provides a quick way to see which pages are linked to other sites outside your own.

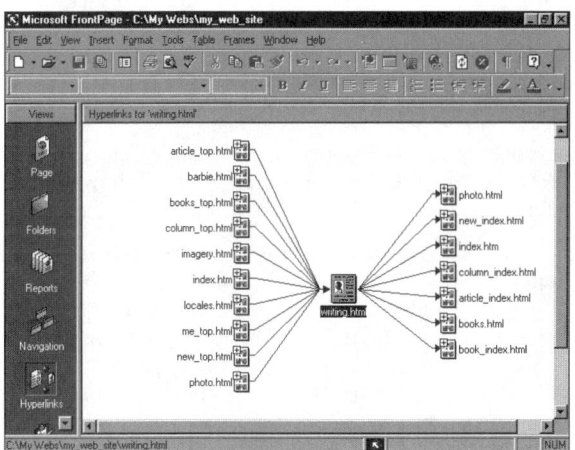

+ **Tasks View:** If you're going to be using FrontPage in a multi-user environment, the Tasks View will no doubt be a common sight. The Tasks View enables you to assign tasks to individuals on your team, check the status of tasks that are already underway, and manage the workflow and the publishing of new elements to the site.

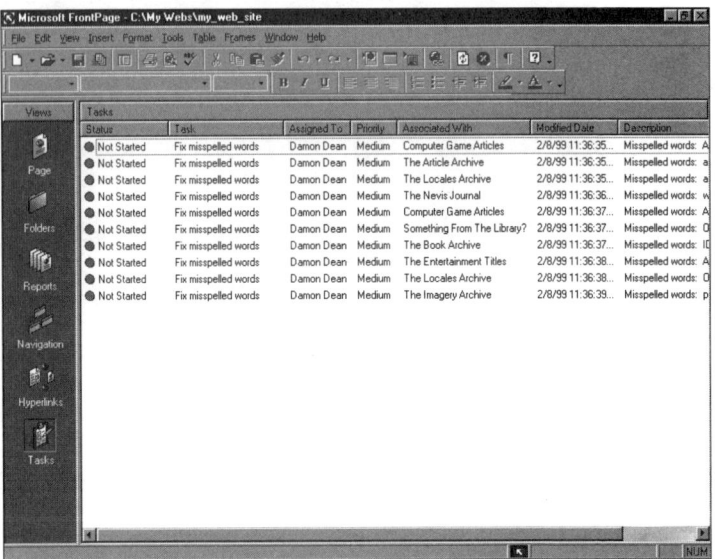

Introducing the FrontPage 2000 Editor

The FrontPage 2000 Editor is the program's built-in tool for creating and viewing Web pages. It's broken into the following three parts (*see* Part IV for more information about each of these modes):

+ **Normal Mode:** Although the meaning of its name is a bit unclear, Normal Mode is actally FrontPage 2000's visual editor for Web development. In Normal Mode, you can place elements — meaning text, graphics, applets, or whatever — on-screen in any location, and FrontPage automatically generates HTML to account for the location of every object.

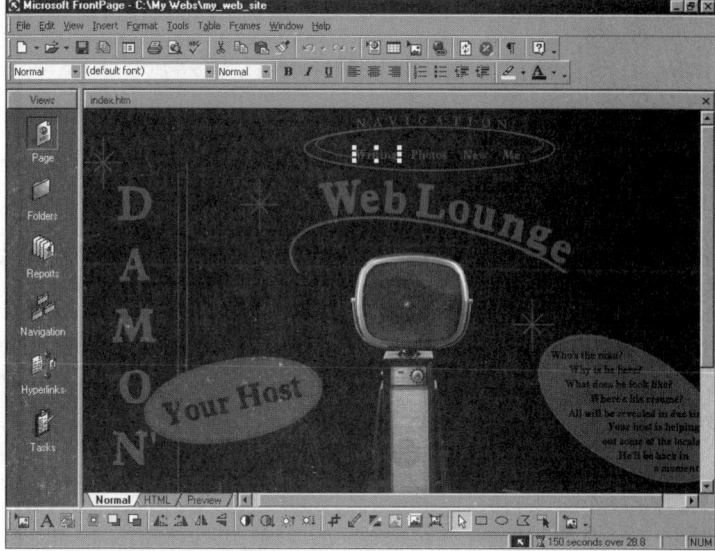

✦ **HTML Mode:** For the purist, HTML Mode enables you to edit raw HTML by hand, just like in the good ol' days.

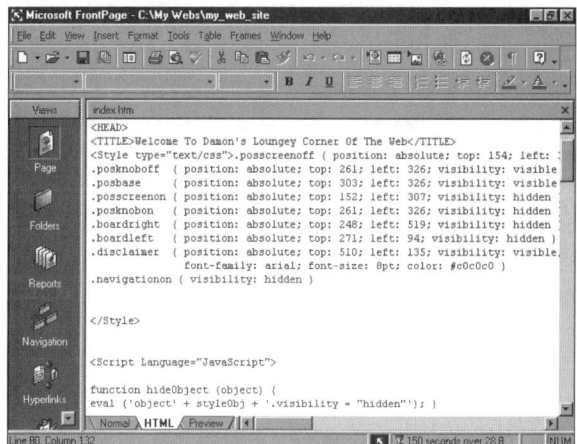

✦ **Preview Mode:** Preview Mode enables you to see what your pages look like in a Web browser window before you put them up on the Internet. FrontPage 2000's default browser is Internet Explorer.

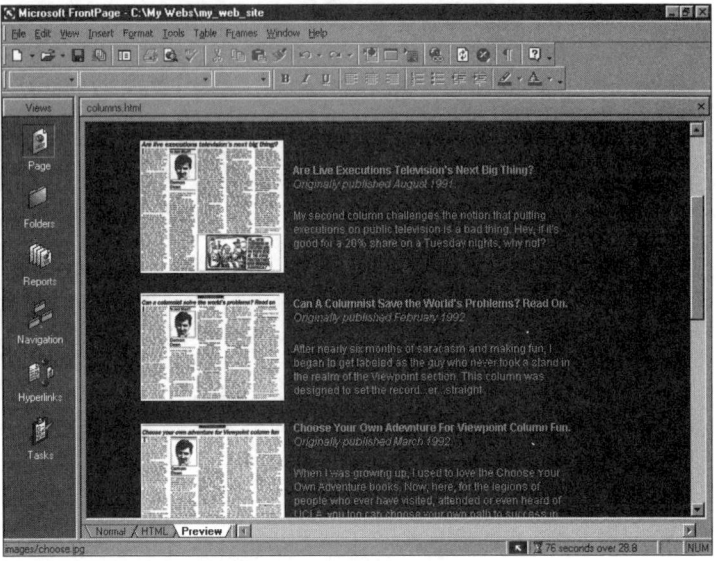

Other FrontPage 2000 Features

In addition to its core features, FrontPage 2000 includes a number of smaller applications that you can use to make the program even more powerful. Many of these "mini-applets" are part of the Microsoft Office family and therefore are embedded in nearly all the Office applications. The following list notes many of the noteworthy mini-applets:

✦ The Microsoft spelling tools, as well as the Thesaurus (*see* Part IV)

✦ Visual Basic Editor

✦ Microsoft Script Editor (*see* Part VII for more on both the Visual Basic Editor and the Microsoft Script Editor)

✦ Add-in support that enables you to access other applications from within FrontPage

✦ Online Help

A Quick Toolbar Rundown

FrontPage 2000 comes with nine different toolbars that you can use to expedite the Web development and publishing processes. Many of these toolbars are common to the Office family, but many others, including the Table Toolbar and the Reports Toolbar, are Web-specific, so you find them only in FrontPage 2000.

See Part III for a complete rundown on how to customize the FrontPage 2000 toolbars.

 In general, using toolbars can save you time because you don't need to worry about searching for the correct menus all the time, nor do you need to continually try to memorize keyboard commands.

The other nice thing about the toolbars is that you can put them nearly anywhere you want. You're probably best off keeping the Standard and Formatting Toolbars in their default positions, but you can move any of the toolbars in FrontPage up to the top of the screen with the default toolbars, or you can float them anywhere else on-screen that you want. That gives you the option to organize them any way you see fit!

Getting Help if You Need It

Inevitably, you're going to need some help getting through the many intricacies of FrontPage 2000, which is probably why you bought this book! Nonetheless, you want to remain aware of the online help features that are accessible in FrontPage 2000. You have the following three basic options for Help:

+ **Help Library:** As do other Office 2000 products, FrontPage 2000 features a large, searchable database of key phrases and topics that can lead you to an answer for your question. To use the FrontPage 2000 Help, choose Help⇨Microsoft FrontPage Help and then click the Contents tab. You can also press F1 to bring up the Help Contents.

+ **The Answer Wizard:** The Answer Wizard is new to FrontPage 2000. You type your question, and the Wizard attempts to provide relevant topics that answer your question. To use the Answer Wizard, choose Help⇨Microsoft FrontPage Help and then click the Answer Wizard tab.

+ **Online Help:** If you're connected to the Internet (and I hope you are!), you can visit the Microsoft Office Help Web site. At the Microsoft Web site, you find up-to-date information about each Office product, as well as a wealth of other resources to help you make the most of FrontPage. To access the site from FrontPage, choose Help⇨Office on the Web, and FrontPage launches your default Web browser.

Part II

The Basics of Webs and Web Pages

You must walk before you can crawl . . . or something like that. If you're just starting out with FrontPage 2000 and don't have much sense of how to tackle the product, don't worry. This part covers some of the more common things you're likely to do with FrontPage Webs and Web pages.

Note: The term *Web* in FrontPage 2000 refers to an entire *Web site*. A *Web page* is an HTML page within a Web. The phraseology is a little confusing, certainly, but those are the terms that FrontPage uses, so you're stuck with them.

In this part . . .

- ✔ Creating Webs
- ✔ Creating Web pages
- ✔ Working with Web files
- ✔ Using templates
- ✔ Importing Webs
- ✔ Saving your work

Changing a Filename

If you're familiar with the way Windows 95/98 allows you to rename files, then FrontPage 2000 will seem awfully familiar, because it works nearly identically. To change the name of a file, follow these steps:

1. If you don't already have the Folder List open, choose View⇨Folder List. The Folder List area appears.

2. Right-click the file in the Folder List that you want to change.

3. Choose Rename from the pop-up menu that appears.

4. Type a new name for the file.

5. Press Enter.

Whenever you change the name of a Web page, you break the links that connect the page to any other pages in your Web site. Fortunately, FrontPage knows exactly how all your Web pages are linked, so when you change the name of a file, FrontPage asks whether you want to automatically update your other pages as well.

If you don't like the whole right-click thing, you can change the Web page's filename another way by following these steps:

1. Choose View⇨Folder List to open the Folder List.

2. In the list, click the name of the file that you want to change.

3. Wait a moment and then click the file's name again. A box appears around the text, the filename is highlighted, and a blinking cursor sits at the end of the filename.

4. Type a new name for the file and press Enter.

Remember: All filenames need either a two-, three-, or four-letter extension. FrontPage reminds you to add the extension if you forget.

Closing Webs and Web Pages

To close your entire Web from any of the FrontPage views, choose File⇨Close Web. Whenever you close a Web, you close any open Web pages as well.

Closing a Web page is slightly different from opening one. You can close a Web page only if you're in the Page View. If you have more than one Web page open and you're in the Page View, you may not see the Web page that you want to close. That's because even though you have more than one page open, the Page View lets you display only one file on-screen at any given time. All the others are hidden.

There are two ways to toggle between all the open Web pages in the Page View:

✦ **Use the Folder List.** If a file is currently open, an icon such as the one you see to the left of this paragraph replaces the standard HTML page icon. If you don't see the HTML page on-screen, just double-click the icon, and FrontPage toggles your Web page to the front so that you can see that page.

✦ **Check the Window menu.** If you choose <u>W</u>indow from the menu bar, all your open Web pages appear in the menu. To switch to a different Web page, click the Web page that you want to view.

After you get to the page that you want, you can close the page by choosing <u>F</u>ile⇨<u>C</u>lose or pressing Ctrl+F4.

Creating a New Web

Whenever you start FrontPage 2000, the program creates a default HTML page, New_page_1.html, and then opens that page for you. Even though FrontPage does some of this work for you, you will want to create your own Web project. To do so, follow these steps:

1. Choose <u>F</u>ile⇨<u>N</u>ew⇨<u>W</u>eb to open the New dialog box, shown in the following figure.

2. Enter the location for your new Web (either on your local machine or on your local network) in the Options area.

3. Select a type of Web from one of the available templates. The templates make possible different kinds of Web sites that you may want to build. The default selection — the one that FrontPage loads on startup — is One Page Web.

   See "Creating a Web from a Template" later in this part for more information about using the FrontPage templates.

4. Click OK or press Enter to create your new Web.

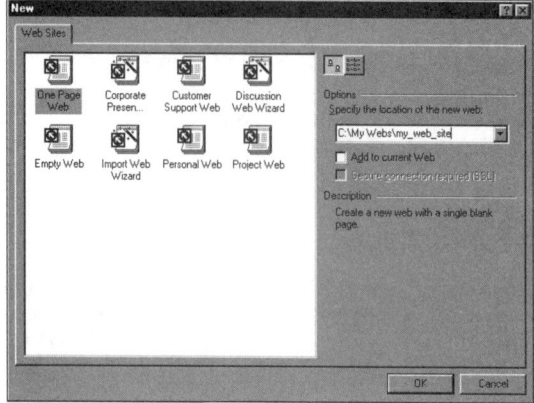

After you create a Web, you can have FrontPage load it automatically on startup by changing the program's options. *See* Part III to find out how to make FrontPage load your Web on startup.

Note: When you create a Web, you'll notice that FrontPage 2000 creates a few "extra items," including an Images folder and a Private folder. The Images folder is the default location for housing images in your Web. The Private folder is where FrontPage puts the majority of its automatically generated code.

Creating a Web from a Template

FrontPage 2000 comes with several Web templates that enable you to design a Web site that you can tailor to your business or personal needs. The following table highlights the features of each template.

Template	Description
One Page Web	Includes just a single Web page.
Corporate Presence Wizard	Includes pages for products and services, feedback, and searching, as well as pages for mission statements and contact information.
Customer Support Web	Includes the tools necessary for building a compelling customer support site, including pages for discussion groups, FAQs, bug-list reports, a searchable database, and bulletin board postings.
Discussion Web Wizard	Includes search forms, a discussion area, and user registration.
Empty Web	Includes only the empty default folders.

Template	Description
Import Web Wizard	Walks you through the process of importing an existing Web into a new Web.
Personal Web	Includes a home page, plus pages for a photo album, your personal interests, and your favorite sites on the World Wide Web.
Project Web	Includes such things as schedules, task status, discussion pages, and team-member information.

Creating Web Pages

Creating new Web pages is perhaps the most common task you perform in FrontPage 2000, especially if you have a good-sized Web site. It's not surprising, then, that FrontPage offers you a plethora of options for generating new Web pages, whether you want to create merely an empty page or something as sophisticated as a page involving frames, embedded Java applets, and Cascading Style Sheets.

See Part VII for more information about Cascading Style Sheets and Java applets.

Creating an empty Web page

You can create a new, empty HTML page to add to your Web in one of the following four ways:

   ✦ **From the File menu:** To create a Web page by using the File menu, choose File⇨New⇨Page. In the New dialog box, select Normal Page and click OK.

 ✦ **From the Standard Toolbar:** Just below the File menu is the New Page toolbar button. Click this button to create a new Web page.

   ✦ **From the Folder List:** Anytime the Folder List is active, you can generate a new, blank Web page by right-clicking a blank part of the Folder List and choosing New Page from the pop-up menu.

   ✦ **From the keyboard:** This may be the easiest method yet! Press Ctrl+N, and the New dialog box appears. Select Normal Page and click OK to generate a new, blank HTML page.

This method works only if you're in the Page View. If you're in the Folders View, pressing Ctrl+N adds a new, blank page, New_page_1.html (and so forth for every new page), to the list of files. In the Navigation View, pressing Ctrl+N creates a new page with the same filename as above. On-screen, however, the HTML page is called New Page 1, which is its title.

Creating a Web page from a template

FrontPage gives you many more options for creating Web pages than just making an empty page. In fact, FrontPage includes 25 different Web page templates that can make it easy for you to choose a Web page that meets your needs.

The following table lists these 25 templates and their key features. To create a Web page from a template in the Page View, press Ctrl+N or choose File⇨New⇨Page to open the New dialog box.

Web Page Template	Features
Bibliography	Creates a page with entries in the correct form for a bibliography.
Confirmation Form	Creates a customer service reply page for users to submit a query.
Feedback Form	Provides a form for submitting and receiving feedback.
Form Page Wizard	Creates a customized page with a form that Web surfers can submit.
FAQ	Includes a blank table of contents and links to major sections (you get to fill them in, however).
Guestbook	Creates a form that visitors can use to post comments to your Web site.
Narrow, Left-aligned Body	Creates a single-column page with text on the left-hand side and a picture on the right-hand side.
Narrow, Right-aligned Body	Creates a single-column page with text on the right and a picture on the left.
One-column Body	Creates a page with a single column in the middle, a title at the top, and some default text down the middle of the page.
One-column Body with Contents and Sidebar	Creates a text column in the middle, a picture on the right, and a blank menu on the left.
One-column Body with Contents on Left	Creates a wide text column along the right and a blank menu on the left.
One-column Body with Contents on Right	Creates a wide text column along the left and a blank menu on the right.
One-column Body with Staggered Sidebars	Creates a text column on the right, with staggered menus on the left.

Web Page Template	Features
One-column Body with Two Sidebars	Creates a text column in the middle, a smaller text column on the right, and a staggered two-column menu on the left.
One-column Body with Two-column Sidebar	Creates one text column on the left, one column of images in the middle, and a blank menu on the right.
Two-column Body	Creates two text columns and a header at the top.
Two-column Body with Contents and Sidebar	Creates two text columns in the middle, a text sidebar on the right, and a blank menu on the left.
Two-column Body with Contents on Left	Creates two text columns to the right and a blank menu on the left.
Two-column Body with Contents on Right	Creates two text columns to the left and a blank menu on the right.
Two-column Staggered Body	Creates two offset text columns down the middle of the page.
Two-column Staggered Body with Contents and Sidebar	Creates two offset text columns down the middle of the page, with a blank menu on the left and a sidebar on the right.
User Registration	Includes a default set of text fields for registering new visitors to your Web site.
Wide Body with Headings	Creates a single, wide text column with headers interspersed after every paragraph of text.
Search Page	Creates a search form with instructions.
Table of Contents	Creates a set of topics and built-in links for your Web pages.
Three-column Body	Creates three columns and a header at the top.

For more information about Web page templates, check out *FrontPage 2000 For Dummies* by Asha Dornfest (published by IDG Books Worldwide, Inc.).

Creating framed Web pages

Ever see a Web page where you can scroll down the page, but the menu at the top never moves and the scrolling page seems to disappear underneath the menu?

A feature known as *frames* controls these nifty tricks — and it's one of the great secrets of HTML. In HTML, you can display more than one Web page on-screen at the same time. A Web page that the user never sees controls the entire process of deciding how many pages appear on-screen, as well as how those pages appear.

In FrontPage 2000, creating framed Web pages is easy! Just follow these steps:

1. In the Page View, choose File⇨New⇨Page from the menu bar. The New dialog box appears.

2. Select the Frames Pages tab.

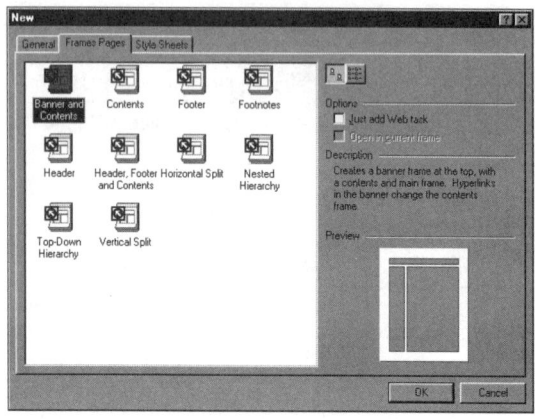

3. Click the style of framed Web page you want. You have ten different frame styles to choose from in FrontPage 2000. After you click a style, a thumbnail preview appears in the bottom-right corner of the dialog box to show you how the frame splits up that Web page.

4. Click OK to generate the framed page.

After you select a style for your framed page, you don't automatically see the page the way it's eventually going to look. When you choose a frame page style, FrontPage 2000 creates a control page for the frame style, leaving the selection of the pages in the frame up to you. On-screen, you see borders breaking up the page according to the frame style you selected. Within each framed area on-screen, you find three long buttons. You use these buttons to select the pages for each framed area in the style you selected. The following figure shows what these buttons look like on-screen after you've created a framed page.

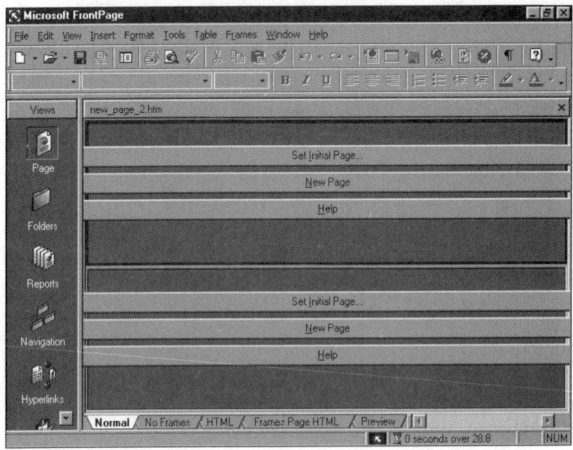

Here's what these buttons do:

✦ **Set Initial Page:** Click this button to select a page in your Web to be included in that framed area.

✦ **New Page:** Click this button to create a new, empty HTML page for that framed area.

✦ **Help:** Click this button to access Microsoft's online help for framed pages.

Want to know more about framed Web pages and how they work? Check out *HTML For Dummies,* 3rd Edition, by Ed Tittel and Stephen N. James (published by IDG Books Worldwide, Inc.).

Importing Webs and Web Pages

If you're working with a number of different Web sites, you may want to import important Web pages, graphics, and even other Web sites into your current Web site. Fortunately, FrontPage 2000 enables you to import such items quite easily.

For importing files into your active Web site, you have the following options:

✦ Import a single file (HTML page, sound file, graphic, applet, or script).

✦ Import the contents of a specific folder.

✦ Import an entire Web.

You must specify the destination into which you want to import files first. To do so, activate the Folder List by choosing View➪Folder List from the menu bar. Then click the folder into which you want to import the data.

Importing a file

To import a file into FrontPage, follow these steps:

1. Choose File➪Import to bring up the Import dialog box.

2. Click the Add File button. The Add File to Import List dialog box appears.

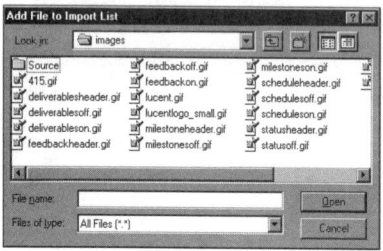

3. Select the file(s) that you want to import from either your local drive or the network.

4. Click the Open button to add the file(s) to your Import List.

5. Click OK in the Import dialog box to import the files into your Web.

Importing a folder

To import a folder into FrontPage, follow these steps:

1. Choose File➪Import to bring up the Import dialog box.

2. Click the Add Folder button to bring up the Browse for Folder dialog box.

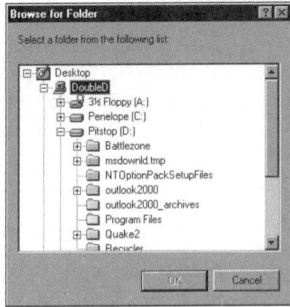

3. Select the folder from which you want to add files by searching through the available local and network drives.

4. Click OK to add that folder and its contents to the Import List.

5. Click OK in the Import dialog box to import the folder into your Web.

You don't have to import files and then import folders separately. You can make a collection of files and folders by adding them to the Import List first. Once you've collected all the items you want to import, click OK in the Import dialog box to import the whole collection.

Importing a Web

To import another Web into your existing FrontPage Web, follow these steps:

1. Choose File⇨Import to bring up the Import dialog box.

2. Click the From Web button to bring up the Import Web Wizard.

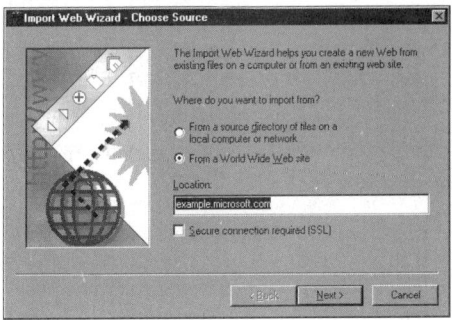

3. Choose the location of the Web you want to import. The wizard provides two simple import options. If you select the From a Source Directory radio button, a Browse button appears on-screen. Click that button to search your local and network drives for available Webs. If you choose the From a World Wide Web Site radio button, the wizard provides a field for you to enter the URL from which you want to import the Web.

4. Click Next to bring up the Choose Download Amount dialog box.

5. Set the download options for the Web you want to import. You can limit the size of the Web you want to download by choosing from a series of check boxes. These check boxes let you specify the number of layers of the Web you want to import, the size (in kilobytes) that you want to import, and the kinds of files you want to import.

6. Click Next to bring up the Finish dialog box.

7. Click the Finish button to import the Web.

Naming Your Web

If you let FrontPage have its way, it names a new Web "My Web." Although this name may seem nice and homey, it isn't particularly effective in helping you remember what your Web contains.

You need to know, too, that after you name your Web, changing the name can prove a hassle. Naming your Web, therefore, can be one of the more important decisions you make.

You name your Web in the New dialog box (shown earlier in this part). In the Options area, in the Specify the Location of the New Web field (catchy name, isn't it?), FrontPage asks you to specify the location of your Web. In fact — and this is confusing — this field determines both the location *and* the name of your new Web. After you name your new Web and click OK, FrontPage 2000 creates a folder with the name you chose, and then it generates the Web contents in that folder.

Although we live in the wonderful world of Windows 95/98/NT, where you can have long filenames that even include spaces between words, I recommend keeping your Web names short. Many servers out there on the Internet (that is, those still using DOS and UNIX syntax . . . ack!) still use the 8.3 filename/extension lengths for their filenames, so the closer you stay to the 8.3 convention, the fewer problems you'll experience.

Opening Files in FrontPage 2000

Because FrontPage 2000 is a part of Microsoft Office, the program can read and edit a large number of different file formats in addition to HTML. Currently, FrontPage supports each of the following file formats:

✦ Web files — HTML, Active Server Pages (ASP), Cascading Style Sheets (CSS), JavaScript, and VB Script files

✦ All Microsoft Office file formats (Word, Excel, Access, and PowerPoint) dating back to Version 2.*x*

✦ Text files

✦ Rich Text files

✦ WordPerfect files going as far back as WordPerfect 5.*x*

✦ Lotus 1-2-3 spreadsheets going back as far as Version 1.*x*

To open a file in FrontPage, follow these steps:

1. Choose File⇨Open to access the Open File dialog box. You can also press Ctrl+O to bring up the Open File dialog box.

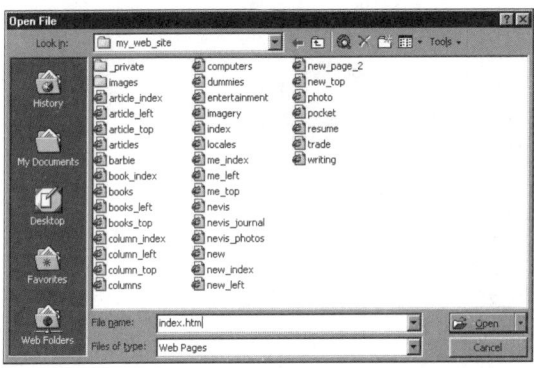

2. Select the file type that you want from the Files of Type drop-down list box.

3. Use the Look In drop-down list to find the file you need.

4. Click the name of the file you want from the list and then click the Open button.

If you can't find the file you're looking for, click the Tools drop-down list (to the far right of the Look In drop-down list), and you can search your hard drive for that renegade file. You can also open a file in a new window by clicking the down arrow on the right side of the Open button. A drop-down list appears. Choose Open in New Window to open the file in a new window.

Retrieving Recent Webs and Web Pages

In FrontPage 2000, your recently revised files are never far away. In fact, they're never farther away than the File menu! To pull up a recently-worked-on file, choose File⇨Recent Files⇨ *Name_of_file*.html. Similarly, to pull up a recently-worked-on Web, choose File⇨ Recent Webs⇨*Name_of_Web*.

In addition to retrieving your files manually, FrontPage can retrieve the last Web you worked on before closing the program. To set this option, follow these steps:

1. Choose Tools⇨Options to open the Options dialog box.

2. Select the General tab.

3. Select the Open Last Web Automatically When FrontPage Starts check box.

4. Click OK.

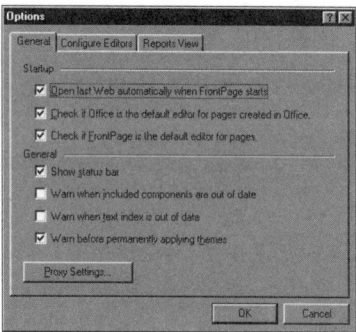

The next time you start FrontPage, the program will open the Web you were working on when you closed the program.

Saving Your Web Pages

There's an old saying in software development circles, and it goes a little something like this: "Save and save often." Ah, I see that you've heard it! Well, saving and saving often is a great idea in FrontPage, too. The number of times you save a file is inversely proportional to how mad you'll get if you lose all the work you just finished.

Keeping that in mind, use one of the following three easy ways to save a file in FrontPage 2000:

+ Choose File➪Save.

+ Click the Save button on the Standard Toolbar.

+ Press Ctrl+S.

If you haven't yet saved the file, the Save As dialog box appears.

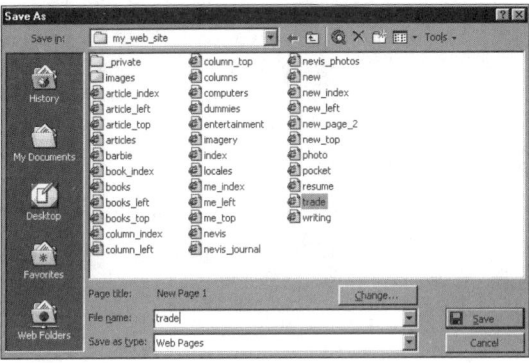

From the Save As dialog box, you can give your file a name and choose where to save it. After you save the file for the first time, you no longer see the Save As dialog box when you use any of the preceding three methods of saving.

Saving an HTML file as a template

Suppose you're working on a Web page and you suddenly realize, "Zoinks! All my other Web pages should have these same basic elements!" With FrontPage 2000, you have the option to save an HTML page as a template, which you can then load like other HTML templates.

To save an HTML page as a template, follow these steps:

1. Choose File⇨Save As. The Save As dialog box appears.

2. In the Save In drop-down list box, select the FrontPage 2000 Template directory. FrontPage 2000 usually resides in `C:\Program Files\Microsoft Office\Templates\1033\Pages`, but the actual location of your program files depends on where you installed your version of FrontPage 2000.

3. Select FrontPage Template (*.tem) from the Save As Type drop-down list.

4. Click the Save button.

After you save your file, you'll be able to see and choose your new template in the New Page dialog box. (See the section "Creating a Web page from a template," earlier in this part.)

Saving a duplicate version of a file

You may need a backup version of a file. Or perhaps you're not sure whether something's going to work right with the latest version of a file, and you don't want to risk messing up your file by making changes to it. The Save As function is kinda handy in these situations.

To make a duplicate version of a file, follow these steps:

1. Choose File⇨Save As. The Save As dialog box appears.

2. From the Save-In drop-down list box, choose a location for the duplicate version of your file.

3. Give the duplicate file a new name.

Remember: In saving your files under a new name, don't delete any of the extension letters after the period (.). Other- wise, FrontPage may not recognize the file type.

4. Click the Save button to save your duplicate version of the file.

Part III

Working with FrontPage 2000 Projects

Cracking open a copy of FrontPage 2000 is a little bit like opening up a new VCR at Christmas: Suddenly, there are a lot of new features and buttons on the controller that you've never seen before. Metaphorically speaking, this part shows you exactly how to program the VCR, set the clock, and even turn on the Picture-in-Picture feature. In other words, if your question has to do with your Web project (and isn't about HTML editing or some advanced feature — those are covered in Part IV), you'll probably find the answer here.

In this part . . .

- ✔ Building Webs by using themes
- ✔ Changing your Web options
- ✔ Publishing a Web site to the Internet
- ✔ Recalculating hyperlinks
- ✔ Assigning tasks
- ✔ Working in the Navigation View

Adding Categories

If you're using FrontPage 2000 in a multi-user collaborative work environment, you can use categories to group Web pages into more usable and relevant topics. For example, imagine that certain pages in a Web — say, job listings — are going to be touched only by the Human Resources department. Categorizing those pages together helps the person charged with overseeing the upkeep of those pages (who may not be all that Web literate) find and edit only the pages that he or she needs to.

You can add categories or statuses to a Web only if you have administration privileges. For more information about permissions, check out "Setting Permissions" later in this part.

To add categories to your Web, follow these steps:

1. Right-click any HTML page or graphics file in the Folders View and then choose Properties from the pop-up menu that appears. This activates the Properties dialog box for that object, as shown in the following figure.

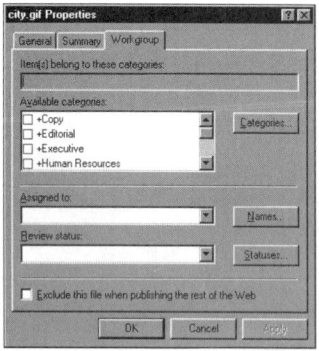

2. Select the Workgroup tab of the Properties dialog box.

As an administrator, you can change the properties associated with anything in the Web, so it doesn't really matter what object you activate the Workgroup tab from, because you'll always be able to edit the categories. Depending on the kind of Web you've created, categories may or may not already appear in the Categories list. You can add others or delete the ones that are already there.

3. Click the Categories button to activate the Master Category List, as shown in the following figure.

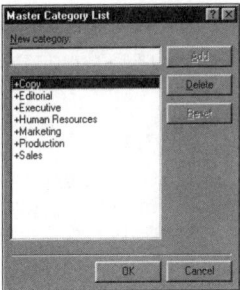

4. In the New Category field, type the name of the category that you want to add.

5. Click the Add button to add the new category or status to the Category list.

6. Click OK to return to the Properties dialog box.

7. Click OK or Cancel to close the Properties dialog box.

Adding Review Statuses

Review Status is a handy way for developers to track the progress of a Web page, graphic object, or any other element in a Web as it makes its way through the production process and out onto the Internet.

You can add statuses to a Web only if you have administration privileges. For more information about permissions, check out "Setting Permissions" later in this part.

Here's how to add review statuses to your Web:

1. Right-click any HTML page or graphics file in the Folders View and then choose Properties from the pop-up menu that appears. This activates the Properties dialog box for that object.

2. Select the Workgroup tab of the Properties dialog box. Depending on the kind of Web you've created, a preset status name such as Complete or In review may already be accessible from the Review Status drop-down list.

3. Click the Statuses button to open the Master Status list.

4. In the New Review Status field, type the name of the review status that you want to add.

5. Click the Add button to add the new status to the Review Status list.

6. Click OK to return to the Properties dialog box.

7. Click OK or Cancel to close the Properties dialog box.

Applying a New Theme to a Web

Themes are compelling graphics and varying text styles that help provide a common look and feel for your Web. FrontPage 2000 comes with more than 60 different themes that you can apply to individual pages, as well as to an entire Web.

To add a theme to a Web or Web page, follow these steps:

1. Choose Format⇨Theme to open the Themes dialog box.

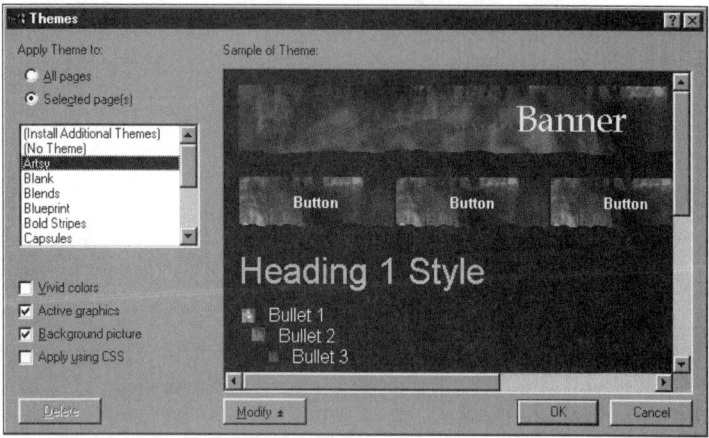

2. Click the theme that you want. The four check boxes that occupy the bottom-left corner of the Themes dialog box give you the following additional options:

• **Vivid Colors:** Uses more vibrant colors as you create your theme graphics and text.

• **Active Graphics:** Creates more interesting and dynamic-looking graphics for such elements as your banner.

• **Background Picture:** Adds a background image to the pages.

• **Apply Using CSS:** Uses Cascading Style Sheets instead of HTML to create your text and graphics styles.

3. To choose any of these options, click the check box next to the text that describes the option that you want.

4. Click OK to apply your chosen theme.

Assigning Review Status to an Object

When it comes time to track the status of an object through the production process, FrontPage 2000 has the tools to help. Here's how to assign a status to any object in your Web:

1. Right-click the HTML page, graphic, sound file, script, or whatever object to which you want to assign a category; then choose Properties from the pop-up menu. This brings up the Properties dialog box specific to that object.

2. Select the Workgroup tab of the Properties dialog box.

3. From the Review Status drop-down list, select the status that you want to assign to the object.

4. Click OK to assign the object the status that you selected.

See also "Adding Review Statuses" earlier in this part.

Assigning Shared Borders to Web Pages

Say that you have a logo that appears at the top of every Web page on your site. Or suppose you have a copyright notice that needs to appear at the foot of each page. By using the FrontPage 2000 Shared Borders feature, you can easily make changes to these kinds of elements across a number of pages.

Shared Borders enables you to designate a region of a Web page as *shared* and then make changes to that region on just one page. FrontPage automatically makes the change on every other page with the same shared border.

To assign a shared border to a series of pages, follow these steps:

1. Click the Folders icon in the Views Bar to access the Folders View. Or if you want to remain in another view, choose View⇨Folders to access the Folders List.

2. Select the pages that you want to have shared borders by holding down the Ctrl key and clicking each page once.

If you're just getting started on your Web, create a number of blank pages first and then select them all to apply a shared border. Then you can streamline your HTML editing from the get-go!

3. Choose Format⇨Shared Borders from the menu bar to open the Shared Borders dialog box.

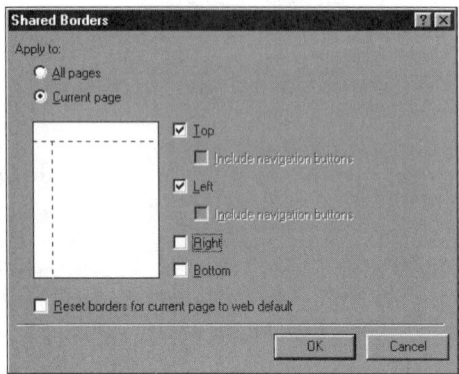

4. Select the region or regions that you want to be shared across the pages. To apply a shared region across all the pages in your Web, select All Pages in the Apply To area of the dialog box.

5. Click OK to share the regions that you've chosen.

Now, if you make any changes to this region on one page, FrontPage automatically makes those changes across every page with the same shared border.

Categorizing an Object

To categorize an object, follow these steps:

1. Right-click the HTML page, graphic, sound file, script, or whatever object to which you want to assign a category; then choose Properties from the pop-up menu. This brings up the Properties dialog box specific to that object.

You can also get to the Properties dialog box by choosing File⇨Properties from the menu bar.

2. Select the Workgroup tab of the Properties dialog box.

3. From the available list of categories, check the boxes next to the categories that you want the object to be part of. Notice that, when you click a category, it gets added to the Item(s) Belong to These Categories field.

4. Click OK to assign the object to those categories.

See also "Adding Categories" earlier in this part.

Changing Web Settings

Your Web comes with a number of settings that you can nip, tuck, and tweak to make your Web look and feel like that comfy old chair sitting in the family room. Okay, so maybe I'm exaggerating, but FrontPage does let you configure a number of your Web's elements. Choose Tools⇨Web Settings to access these options.

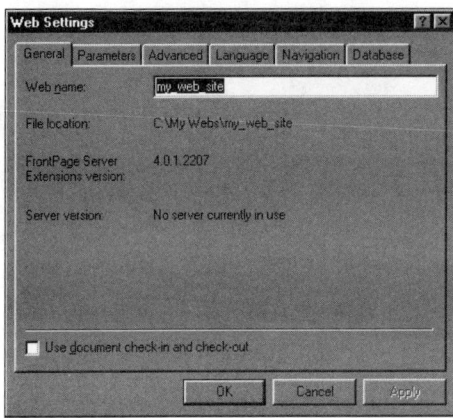

The following table lists some of the basic settings that you can change in the Web Settings dialog box and the tabs on which they appear.

Setting	Tab Location
Change the name of a Web	General
Enable source control	General
Change the default scripting language	Advanced
Show documents in hidden directories	Advanced
Delete temporary files	Advanced
Change the server messaging language	Language
Change the default page encoding	Language
Customize text labels for autogenerated navigation bars	Navigation

Adding a database connection to a Web

Although the Web Settings dialog box may seem a strange place for adding a database, it includes a tab for doing just that. A database can house many types of information and can be used to provide a very interactive experience for the visitors to your Web site.

Check out *Access For Windows For Dummies* by John Kaufeld (published by IDG Books Worldwide, Inc.) for more information about using databases.

To add a database to your Web from the Web Settings dialog box, follow these steps:

1. Choose Tools⇨Web Settings from the menu bar to bring up the Web Settings dialog box.

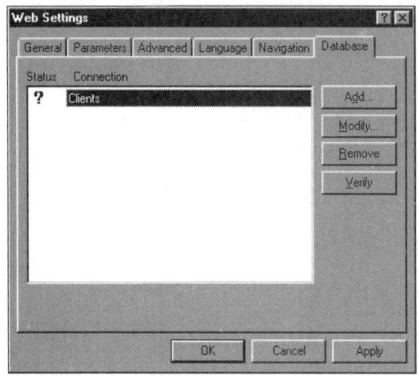

2. Select the Database tab. This tab contains your status area, which you will eventually check to make sure that the database is active and running. Assuming that you haven't loaded any databases yet, this area should be empty.

3. Click Add to add a new database to your Web. The New Database Connection dialog box appears.

4. In the Name field, type a name for the database to which you want to connect.

5. Select the location from which you're going to connect your database by selecting one of three radio buttons in the Location of Database area. Your choices include the following:

• **File or Folder in Current Web:** Select this button to find a database that's already within your Web.

• **Data Source on Web Server:** Select this button if the database you want to connect to is on the Web server where your Web resides.

• **Other Database Server on the Network:** Select this button if the database you want to activate is a server other than the one to which your Web is connected.

TIP

You can click the Advanced button to access the Advanced Database Connection Properties dialog box and review the advanced settings for connecting to a database. From this dialog box, you can specify any required elements in connecting to the database, such as a user ID or password, timeout settings, and parameters (string variables) that you want to be able to pass to the database.

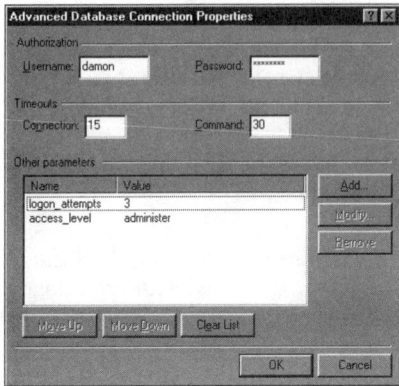

6. Click the Browse button to select the location of the database to which you want to connect. Based on your selection in the preceding step, FrontPage provides the appropriate dialog box to connect to a database for these three connection types:

• **File or Folder in Current Web:** Here, FrontPage 2000 brings up the Database Files In Current Web dialog box. Using the drop-down list, you can browse through the active Web to find available databases. After you find the appropriate file, click the database file and then click OK to add the database connection and return to the Database tab of the Web Settings dialog box.

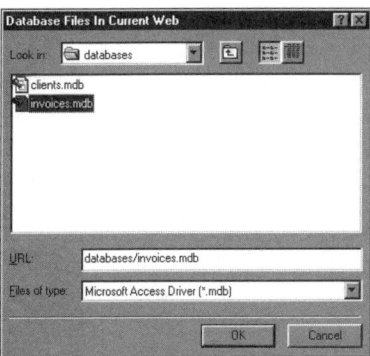

• **Data Source on Web Server:** If you choose this option, FrontPage 2000 searches the active Web server that houses your Web (if you're using Microsoft Personal Web Server, this may be your local drive) and tells you of any active databases on that server. Click the database file and then click OK to add the database connection and return to the Database tab of the Web Settings dialog box.

• **Other Database Server on the Network:** If you choose this option, you get the Network Database Connection dialog box. Here, you choose your database type (there are only two: SQL server and Microsoft ODBC for Oracle) from the Type of Database drop-down list. Then type the server's URL in the Server Name field and include the name of the database in the Database Name field. Click OK to add the database connection and return to the Database tab of the Web Settings dialog box.

Databases are a big undertaking and not something to take lightly. If you're just getting started with FrontPage 2000, you may want to shy away from databases for the moment and stick to the basics.

7. Click OK in the Web Settings dialog box to add the database connection to your Web.

Adding parameters to a Web

Parameters let you specify a variable for your Web project and then retrieve that variable in the FrontPage Editor while you're building pages. This feature is especially handy if you're repeating chunks of information — such as an address, some product information, or a hyperlink — throughout the site.

To add a parameter to your Web, follow these steps:

1. Choose Tools⇨Web Settings from the menu bar. This brings up the Web Settings dialog box.

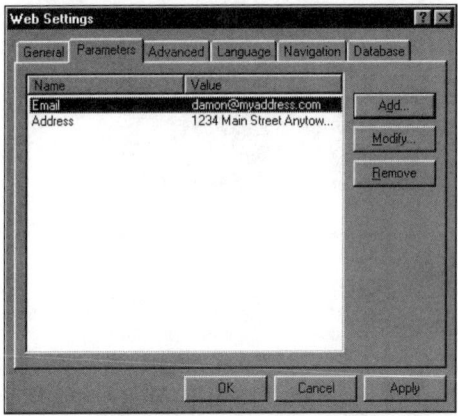

2. From the Parameters tab, click the A̲dd button.

3. Choose an easy-to-remember name for your new variable and enter it under N̲ame in the large text box of the Parameters tab.

4. In the V̲alue box, enter the data that you want to appear on your Web page after you retrieve the variable.

5. Click OK to set the parameter in your Web.

FrontPage 2000 won't let you use a colon in the name that you give a variable. All the other characters are okay to use, however.

If you want a variable that's more than one line long, press Ctrl+Enter to get a carriage return in the Variable field. If you just press Enter, FrontPage puts you back out to the Web Settings dialog box.

Checking Spelling throughout a Web

In FrontPage, you can run a Web-wide spell-check to see which pages contain spelling errors. You can also tell FrontPage to fix those spelling errors and track them so that you can see them in the Tasks View. To track spelling errors in FrontPage, follow these steps:

1. From the Folders View, choose T̲ools⇨S̲pelling. The Spelling dialog box appears. (As with other Office products, you can also press F7 to open the Spelling dialog box.)

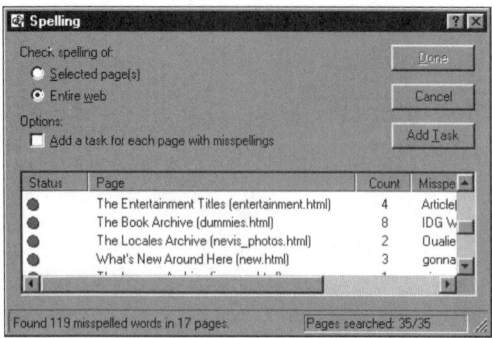

2. Choose whether you want to run a spell-check on the Entire Web or on only Selected Page(s) by selecting one of the two radio buttons in the dialog box.

3. Select the Add a Task for Each Page with Misspellings check box to turn those spelling mistakes into tasks. (*See* "Creating Tasks" later in this part for more information about using tasks.)

4. Click OK. FrontPage checks through all the files you specified and provides you with a report on the pages that contain spelling errors, as well as the number of spelling errors on those pages.

See "Using the Spell Checker and Thesaurus" in Part IV for more information about spelling features in the FrontPage HTML editor.

Collapsing and Expanding Folders

FrontPage 2000 employs many of the same features that reside in Windows 95, Windows 98, and Windows NT. Among these features is the capability to view data through collapsing and expanding folders. In FrontPage, you can view your Web pages, images, and folders from any of the FrontPage views except the Reports View and the Tasks View.

To take advantage of this handy way to view your Web site, follow these steps:

1. Activate the Folders List by choosing View➪Folder List.

2. Click any folder with a plus sign surrounded by a box to expand the folder and view the contents of that folder. After you click the plus sign, you'll notice that it changes to a minus sign surrounded by a box.

3. To collapse the folder, click the minus sign surrounded by a box.

In FrontPage, you can also copy and move files by using the Folders List, just as you can in the Windows Explorer. Simply right-click the file, drag it into the desired folder, and choose either Copy or Move from the pop-up menu.

Configuring Editors

FrontPage 2000 can handle a lot of different file types, but it can't handle all of them. If you're adding a WAV file to your Web site, for example, and you want to be able to edit the WAV file by using a sound editor, you need to tell FrontPage to launch that editor when the file is double-clicked.

Follow these steps to add an editor:

1. Choose Tools⇨Options to open the Options dialog box.

2. Select the Configure Editors tab. You see the following screen showing the programs that you've assigned to edit various file types.

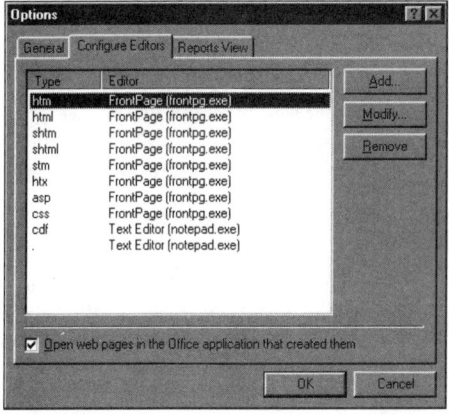

3. Click the Add button to add an associated editor. The Add Editor Association dialog box appears and asks you to specify the *file extension* (the three- or four-letter designation that comes after the period in the file's name), a name for the editor, and the location of the program (in the Command field). If you don't know the location of the editor program you want to use, click the Browse button and search for the program manually.

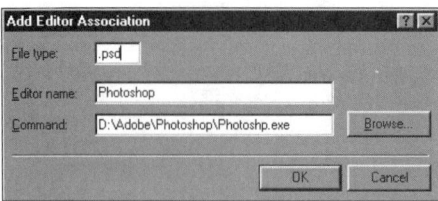

4. Click OK to activate the editor association.

In addition to adding editors, you can also edit the properties of an existing editor, as well as remove editor associations, in the same dialog box. To remove an editor, click the association on the Configure Editors tab of the Options dialog box and then click the Remove button.

Copying Files to a Web

FrontPage 2000 works like the Windows Explorer, so copying files into a Web may seem awfully familiar. Here's how you copy files:

1. Resize your FrontPage window so that you can toggle between your desktop and the application by pressing Alt+Tab.

2. Activate the Folder List by choosing View⇔Folder List. Or you can click the Folders icon in the Views Bar or choose View⇔ Folders to toggle between your desktop and the application.

3. On your computer, locate the folder that includes the file that you want to add to your Web.

4. From that folder, drag the desired file into the Folder List window in FrontPage and place it in the folder where you want the file to go. You know that you can copy your chosen file to your Web after you see the plus sign surrounded by a box beneath the pointer cursor.

Remember: You can drag files by using the right mouse button instead of the left. The advantage? You can cancel your operation if you decide that you really don't want that file in your Web.

See "Importing Webs and Web Pages" in Part II to find out how to use the Import command to copy files to your Web.

Creating Folders

FrontPage 2000 offers you two ways to create new folders for a Web project. The easiest way is to go to the Folders View and choose File⇨New⇨Folder from the menu bar. In this case, FrontPage generates the new folder in the directory that's currently selected in the Folders View.

Switching back over to the Folders View to create a new folder isn't always convenient, however. Fortunately, you can generate new folders in any of the views in which you can bring up the Folder List. Here's how you do it:

1. If the Folder List is not already open, choose View⇨Folder List to activate it.

2. Right-click the folder in which you want to place your new folder and then choose New Folder from the pop-up menu that appears. FrontPage creates the new folder and prompts you to enter a name for it.

3. Enter a name for your new folder in the active text box next to your new folder. The text box appears as a black box with a blinking white cursor at the end of the box.

4. Press Enter to set the name of your new folder.

Creating Tasks

FrontPage uses a task-driven project management system to track how you conduct your work on a Web site in both single- and multi-user environments. Whew! Now that's a mouthful! Believe me, however: creating a task isn't as cumbersome as it may appear in print. Basically, tasks are fancy-looking to-do lists.

You can add a task to any object in a FrontPage Web, and also apply tasks to functions within a Web — a spell-check, for example. There are a few ways to add a task in FrontPage. Here's the skinny on each method:

✦ **Adding a task from the pull-down menus:** This is the mundane way, but it works. To add a task from the File menu, choose File⇨New⇨Task. You can also add a task from the Edit menu by choosing Edit⇨Task⇨Add Task.

✦ **Adding a task from the Task View:** In the Task View, you can add a task by right-clicking anywhere on the active window and choosing New Task from the pop-up menu.

✦ **Adding a task from any other view:** Adding a task from the other views is nearly identical to adding a task in the Task View. The difference is that here you have to right-click your file to get the pop-up menu and then choose Add Task.

If you create a task, you get a New Task dialog box similar to the one shown in the following figure. If you click an item and then add a task, an association with that file automatically appears in the Associated With line of the dialog box. Otherwise, the line remains blank.

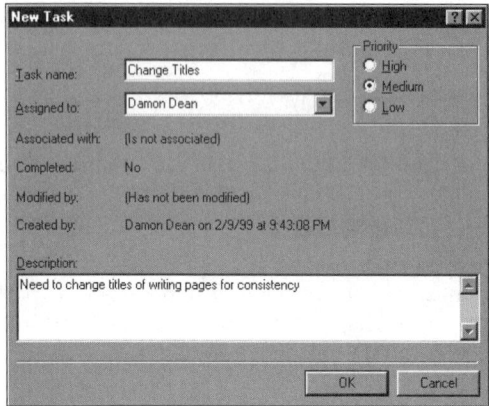

Deleting Files and Folders

FrontPage 2000 offers a number of ways for you to delete files and folders. To delete any file or folder from your project, choose from any of the following methods:

+ **Deleting from the Folder List:** Click an item and press Delete. The Confirm Delete dialog box appears to make sure that you're really serious about wanting to delete the file or folder.

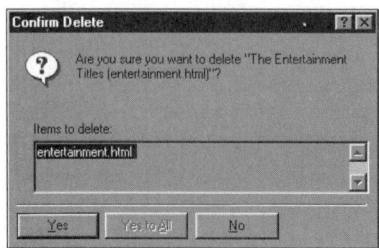

+ **Deleting from the Folder View:** This procedure works just like the Folder List option that I described in the preceding paragraph.

+ **Deleting from the Reports menu:** You can also delete various HTML pages on which you generate reports. Just click the HTML page in a report and press Delete. Again, the Confirm

Delete dialog box appears to confirm that you want to delete the HTML page. You can't do this from the Site Summary report, however.

✦ **Deleting from the Navigation View:** Deleting from this view is slightly different. Select the page that you want to delete and then press Delete. The Delete Page dialog box appears, as the following figure shows. Select the Remove This Page and All the Pages Below It from All Navigation Bars radio button to keep the page in the Web but delete all links to the file, or select the Delete This Page and All the Pages Below It from the Web radio button to eliminate the page entirely.

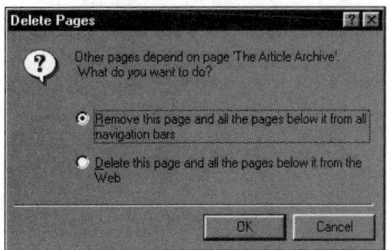

✦ **Deleting from the Hyperlinks View:** Select the page that you want to delete and press the Delete key. The Confirm Delete dialog box appears to make sure that you want to delete your selection.

✦ **Deleting from drop-down lists:** This option is available whenever you have a file selected. To delete the selected file, you can either press the Delete key or choose Edit⇨Delete.

After you delete a page from your Web, you can't undo the action. You're always better off eliminating the page from the active Web by stripping the page out of the Navigation View first and then removing the page. This method eliminates the file from use, but at least keeps it in the Web. That way, you can check to see whether deleting it had any unintended repercussions. The same rule applies for other kinds of files as well.

Editing a Theme

What if you like the look of a theme, but the color just doesn't work for you? Thankfully, FrontPage lets you be as picky as you want. You can almost endlessly modify any of the more than 60 themes in FrontPage, providing hours of fun for the entire family!

Here's how you modify a theme:

1. Choose Format⇨Theme to open the Themes dialog box.

2. Click the theme that you want.

3. Click the Modify button. The new level of options that appears gives you the option to change the colors, graphics, and/or text of your theme.

4. Click the Colors, Graphics, or Text button to edit the color, graphic, and text properties of your theme.

5. Click the Save button to save any changes to the theme, or click the Save As button to save your theme under a new name. If you click the Save As button, the Save Theme dialog box appears. Choose a new name for your theme and then click OK to save the new theme.

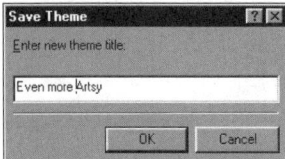

Editing theme colors

You can edit as little or as much as you like of the color properties for every theme in FrontPage 2000. You can edit the properties in three different ways, all of which you can access by clicking the Colors button in the Themes dialog box (see Step 3 in the preceding section). This takes you to the Modify Theme dialog box, where you can modify your color schemes by using one of the following methods:

✦ **Changing color schemes:** FrontPage 2000 includes 55 (yes, I counted them!) different color combinations that you can apply to a theme, in addition to a custom color scheme that you can select yourself. To specify a color scheme, just click the name of the scheme on the Color Schemes tab and then click OK in the Modify Theme dialog box.

✦ **Changing the Color Wheel:** After you select a color scheme, you can play with it even more by selecting the Color Wheel tab. By using the Color Wheel, you can assign a primary color to the theme from more than 32,000 different RGB colors by selecting a color on the wheel. FrontPage then reassembles the rest of the theme based on your primary color selection. You can also use the slider bar — also on the Color Wheel tab — to adjust the brightness of the theme colors. To adjust the brightness of the color selection, click and drag the slider bar to the left to make it less bright and to the right to make it brighter.

✦ **Choosing custom settings:** Each theme is made up of 14 different color properties, which apply to things like the color of hyperlinks or body text. FrontPage lets you modify the color for each of these 14 elements within a theme. You can do so by selecting the Custom tab of the Modify Theme dialog box, selecting the element from the Item drop-down list, and then assigning a color to it from the Color drop-down list.

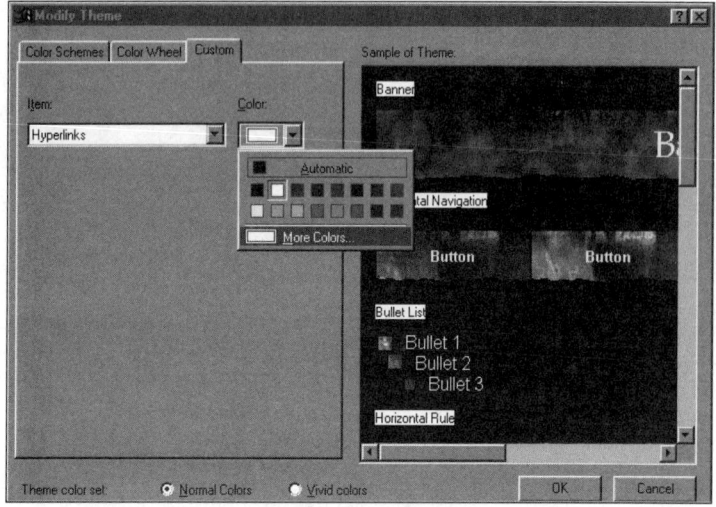

Editing theme graphics

You can edit 11 graphics properties associated with any theme if you click the Graphics button in the Themes dialog box. Remember, though, that you need to click the Modify button in the Themes dialog box in order to see the Graphics button! Properties for graphics that you can change from the Modify Theme dialog box include background graphics, banners, and navigational components, to name just a few.

To edit any of these graphics properties, follow these steps:

1. Choose the graphic property that you want to edit from the Item drop-down list of the Modify Theme dialog box for graphics.

2. Select the Picture tab to edit the graphic you're using for the specific theme element that you want to edit. Some elements contain more than one embedded graphic. You can add your own graphics manually or use the Browse button to find the location of the graphics file that you want on your desktop.

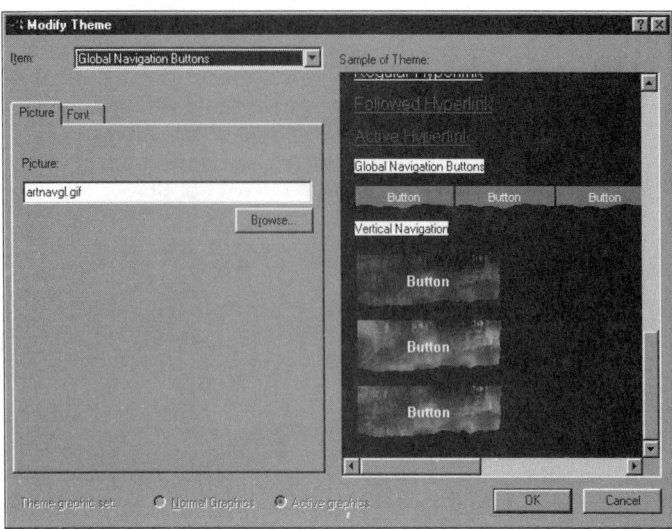

3. Select the Font tab to edit any text properties associated with the selected element in the Item drop-down list. If the item is an editable text element, your choices in the Font tab are available for selection and include Font Type, Style, Size, Horizontal Alignment, and Vertical Alignment.

Although you can access all the fonts on your PC from the Font tab, you should stick with Arial and Times New Roman, because these are Web-standard fonts that every browser supports and nearly all users have on their computers.

4. Select either the Normal Graphics or Active Graphics radio button at the bottom of the dialog box. The basic difference between Normal Graphics and Active Graphics is that Active Graphics have more of a pseudo-3D quality to them.

5. Click OK to make the changes to the theme and return to the Themes dialog box. From there, click OK again to implement the theme changes to your Web.

Editing theme text

Many theme text elements include embedded graphics, but a number of them — seven, to be exact — don't contain any graphics at all. You can edit those seven text styles by clicking the Text button in the Themes dialog box. Remember, though, that you need to click the Modify button in the Themes dialog box in order to see the Text button! When you click the Text button, you get the Modify Theme dialog box for text, where you can edit the properties for the seven text categories.

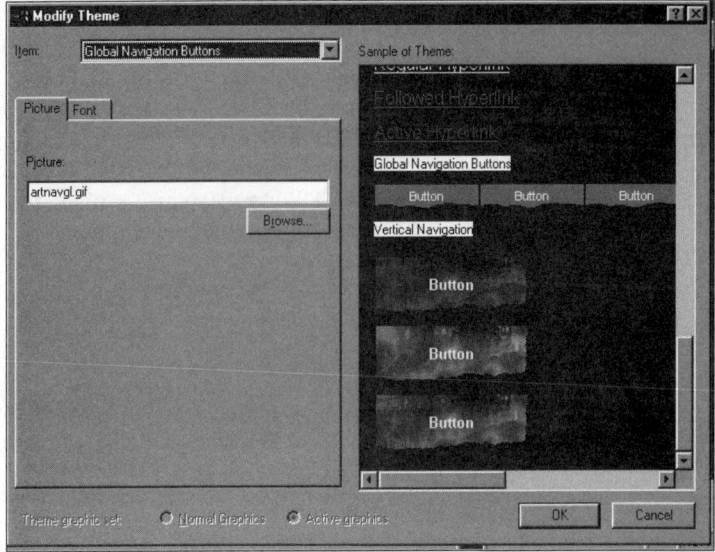

See "Editing theme graphics" earlier in this part for details on which properties are editable from the Modify Theme dialog box.

In addition to the seven text categories, you can also specify a text style for all the Cascading Style Sheet elements and other HTML tags that FrontPage 2000 supports for each theme. Although it's tedious and is not recommended, you can click the More Text Styles button to specify this information.

See Part VII for more information about Cascading Style Sheets.

Finding Things in Your Web

A Web can be pretty big place. That's why the Find function exists: to help you navigate through your Web. In FrontPage 2000, you can search through individual files for a particular word or phrase, or you can search the entire Web if you like and let FrontPage do all the work.

To search through your Web for a word or phrase, follow these steps:

1. Activate the Folder List by choosing View➪Folder List. (You can also switch from your active view to the Folders View by clicking the Folders button on the Views Bar.)

2. Select the folder in which you want to conduct the file search. To search your entire Web, select the root directory file folder. The root directory file folder's name is the same as your Web.

So, for example, if you named your Web "MyWeb," you would select the MyWeb folder to search through your entire Web.

3. Choose Edit➪Find to open the Find dialog box. Type what it is you're looking for in the Find What field. Select one of the options from the Find dialog box to either expand or restrict your search. You can make your search case-sensitive or restrict the search to whole words, for example, by selecting those check boxes in the Find dialog box.

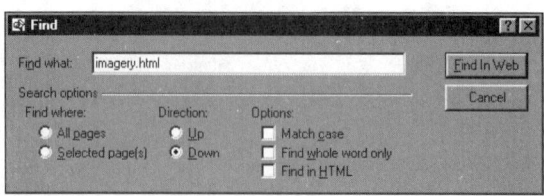

Note: Although FrontPage is consistent with Windows Explorer in many other areas, you can't find files in FrontPage in the same manner as in Windows Explorer. Unlike in Windows Explorer, you can't use the * (asterisk) key in FrontPage to expand your search parameters.

4. Click the Find in Web button to begin your search. Search results include the status of the Web page, the last person to modify the Web page, and the number of times FrontPage found the search item on the Web page. If you double-click a search result, FrontPage immediately sends you to that page.

Moving Project Pages

You can move your Web pages around outside of FrontPage in the Windows Explorer, but that really isn't a good idea. Why? Well, what if those pages contain hyperlinks? If you move your pages outside of FrontPage, Windows sure as heck isn't going to update those links for you! Moving your pages inside FrontPage, however, is another story.

Moving pages around is mostly a tool for organizing your data. With the FrontPage Folders View, moving pages is a snap. Here's how you do it:

1. Activate the Folders View by choosing View➪Folders.

2. Click the file that you want to copy in the Contents Of area. This area includes both files and folders. After you double-click a folder, the Contents Of area shows you the contents of that folder and displays the name of the folder at the top. If you want to see a folder that's back a level from your current folder, press the Backspace key.

3. Drag the file that you want to copy from the Contents Of window to the folder in the Folder List to which you want to copy the file. As the new file moves into the new folder, FrontPage recalculates the hyperlinks associated with that file so that they stay with the file, as shown in the following figure.

See "Creating New Folders" earlier in this part for more information about moving project pages.

Organizing Project Pages

FrontPage provides a visual method for viewing your Web site through the Navigation View (see the following figure). Visually, FrontPage's method for viewing files is slightly akin to an organizational chart. Functionally, organizing your pages is an exercise in dragging pages around and establishing relationships between pages so that your site makes more sense to you and to others who may be working on it.

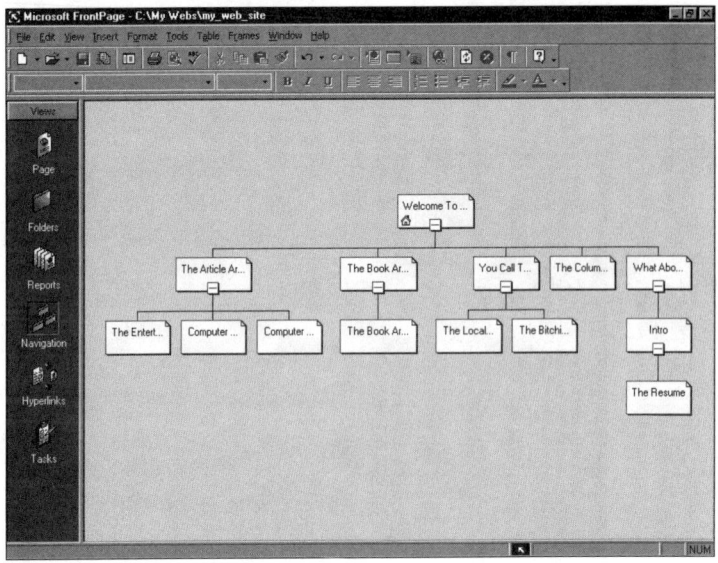

In addition to providing a visual representation of your Web site, the Navigation View also provides a mechanism for generating the appropriate navigation bars for any page in your site, based on the layout that you create.

See "Adding Navigation Bars to Your Web Page" in Part IV for more information about the Navigation View.

Adding Web pages to the Navigation View

The Navigation View is FrontPage 2000's visual organizational tool that enables you to organize the pages of your Web in a meaningful and logical manner. If you want a visual representation of your site, however, you'll undoubtedly have to build it all yourself because FrontPage adds only one page to the Navigation View by default. The program assumes that index.html — no matter what — is always going to be your home page.

To add a Web page to the Navigation View, follow these steps:

1. Activate the Navigation View by choosing View⇨Navigation or by selecting Navigation from the Views Bar.

2. Choose View⇨Folder List to activate the Folder List.

3. Select the Web page that you want to add to the Navigation View and drag it onto the Navigation View window. After you drag a page onto the Navigation View window, FrontPage creates a proxy version of the Web page, along with a virtual link that attaches itself to the closest Web page to the arrow cursor, as shown in the following figure. You can move the proxy version of the page around to other pages that are already in the Navigation View window, and the links change, demonstrating the different relationships between the pages.

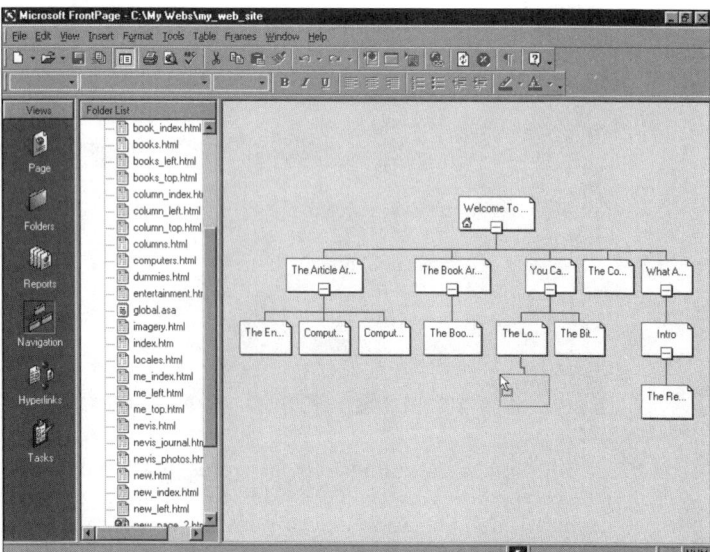

4. Release the mouse button to set the relationship between the page that's closest to the pointer and the page from the Folder List. After a page is in the Navigation View window, you can click and drag the page to a new position. While you still have the page selected and the mouse button depressed, the proxy version of the page and the virtual links appear again and update the position of the page as you move it around on-screen, until you let go of the mouse button.

If you drag a page from the Folder List onto the Navigation View window but don't get the proxy page close enough to a page already in the Navigation View so that FrontPage generates the virtual link, the page will disappear after you release the mouse button.

If your site's getting big, viewing the pages vertically may not be the best way to see your whole site. To view your Web pages horizontally, right-click the Navigation View window background and then choose Rotate. Now all your pages cascade off the Index page from left to right, instead of from top to bottom.

Adding external links in the Navigation View

In addition to creating links between pages within your Web, you can add links to other Web sites. You would want to add links to other Web sites if you were using the Navigation View to generate navigation bars in your Web pages and wanted to include an external site in your navigation menu.

External links can link either to another Web site or to an e-mail that you send. To set an external link in the Navigation View, follow these steps:

1. Right-click any Web page in the Navigation View window and then choose External Hyperlink from the pop-up menu to open the Select Hyperlink dialog box.

2. Enter the URL or e-mail address in the URL text box of the Select Hyperlink dialog box. (To add the e-mail address, click the e-mail icon in the dialog box or type **mailto:** before the e-mail address in the URL text box. You then fill in the address in the Create E-mail Hyperlink dialog box, shown in the following figure.)

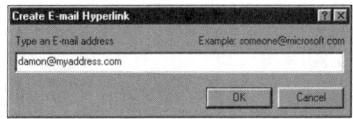

3. Click OK to generate the link.

Printing a schematic of your Web

One of the nice things about the Navigation View is that you have a handy schematic of your entire Web site in front of you at all times. After you get more than, say, 30 pages in the Navigation View, however, getting all those boxes to fit on a single screen becomes nearly impossible. So what if you want to print the thing?

Follow these steps to print your large Web page schematic:

1. Right-click the Navigation View window and choose Zoom⇨ Size to Fit from the pop-up menu to get your entire site to fit on-screen. Size to Fit shrinks the page icons so that they all fit within the Navigation View window. Size to Fit also ensures that, as you print your Web site schematic, the whole schematic fits on a single page.

2. Choose File⇨Print Preview to see what your schematic is going to look like when you print it.

If your schematic still looks too cramped, choose File⇨Page Setup and change the page orientation from Portrait to Landscape.

3. Once you're satisfied with the look of your schematic, choose File⇨Print and click OK in the Print dialog box to print the schematic.

Previewing Web Pages in a Browser

FrontPage 2000 comes with a built-in Web browser, but sometimes, you just can't beat the real thing. In FrontPage, you can preview a Web page in any of the browsers installed on your PC.

To preview a Web page from any browser on your desktop, follow these steps:

1. Switch to the Folders View by clicking the Folders icon in the Views Bar, or choose View⇨Folder List to open the Folder List from your current view.

2. Click the page that you want to preview in an external Web browser.

3. Choose File⇨Preview in Browser from the menu bar. The Preview in Browser dialog box appears.

4. Select the browser in which you want to preview the page. The installed browsers that FrontPage 2000 detects appear in the Browser list. You can add browsers to this list by clicking the Add button, which brings up the Add Browser dialog box. From there, you can name your browser and specify the browser's location in the Command field. If you don't know the location of the browser, click the Browse button to search your local drive for the browser executable.

5. Designate a window size by selecting one of the radio buttons in the Window Size area. FrontPage supports four viewing ranges: the browser Default size, 640 x 480, 800 x 600, and 1024 x 768.

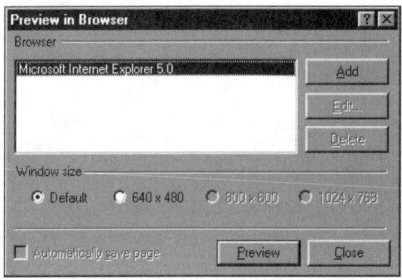

6. Click the Preview button to view your Web page in the specified browser.

Publishing Webs

If you own FrontPage 98 or earlier, you probably know that moving your Web content from your local machine to a Web server was at one time the most convoluted and frustrating experience imaginable.

 Without going into the grim and gory details of previous versions of FrontPage, let me put your mind at ease right here. FrontPage 2000 is much, much better, and nearly all the quirkiness of previous versions of the product has been eliminated. Here's a brief run-down of the ways in which you can publish Web content in FrontPage 2000:

✦ **Connecting directly to a FrontPage server:** This was the preferred method of publishing content in previous versions of FrontPage. In this method, your Web resides on another server, and you do all your editing and publishing in real time while you're connected to your Web on that server.

 While I touch very briefly on how to connect to a FrontPage server, this really is beyond the scope of this book. However, *FrontPage 2000 For Dummies* covers it in depth.

✦ **Publishing by using HTTP:** Also available in previous versions of FrontPage, this method allows you to use the standard World Wide Web file transfer method — HTTP — to move content from your local machine to a FrontPage server on the Internet.

♦ **Publishing by using FTP:** This is the feature that FrontPage users have been screaming for since the product was introduced. Built into FrontPage 2000 is an FTP, or File Transfer Protocol, program that enables you to publish to another server that is not a FrontPage server.

Publishing with both HTTP and FTP are covered later in this part, as are the basics of connecting to a FrontPage server.

Publishing a Web by using HTTP

HTTP sounds new and nifty, but if you've ever loaded a Web page, you already know what HTTP does. HTTP, which stands for HyperText Transfer Protocol, is simply a way of transferring data from a server to your Web browser (and vice versa). In fact, HTTP is the preferred way of transferring files in FrontPage 2000.

 To use this method of file transfer, your Internet service provider must support the FrontPage server extensions.

Here's how you publish a Web by using HTTP:

1. Choose File➪Publish Web. The Publish Web dialog box appears, as shown in the following figure. From this dialog box, you can manage the amount of content you want to publish and specify the Web server on which you want to post it.

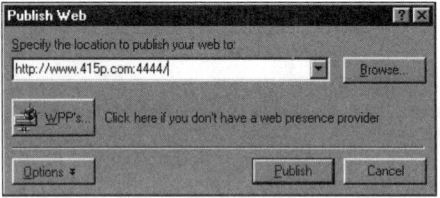

2. Click the Options button. This button reveals other publishing options that you may want to consider. You can choose to publish only those Web pages that change, for example, and you can include other sub-Webs that you include in your site.

3. Enter the URL where you want to publish your Web content in the Specify the Location to Publish Your Web To text box at the top of the dialog box. Click the WPP's button if you're not sure whether your ISP provides the appropriate server extensions to support FrontPage's publishing features. The WPP's button sends you to the Microsoft Web site for the most current list of ISPs that support the extensions.

If you're not sure of the location to which you want to publish your Web, click the Browse button in the Publish Web dialog box to search for FrontPage servers from the Open Web dialog box (yes, that's a bit of a misnomer). You can use the link buttons on the left side of the dialog box or use the drop-down list to look for FrontPage servers on your hard drive, on network drives, or in your Web Folders area.

4. Click Publish to submit the new Web content. FrontPage tracks the progress of the upload and shows you which pages are being transferred. Once the upload is complete, an alert box appears telling you that the upload is done.

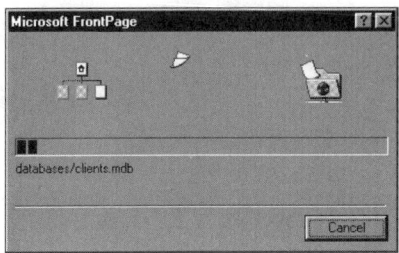

 If you're publishing your Web to a Web server, there's a pretty good chance that it's password protected. When you first see the Publish Web dialog box, you're more likely than not going to get another dialog box prompting you for your user name and password. This is to prevent people from coming along and posting content on any Web site they want.

 Always, *always* double-check your Web site after you upload new content to make sure that the new content got there all in one piece!

Setting up an FTP location

To set up an FTP connection, follow these steps:

1. Choose File⇨Open Web to bring up the Open Web dialog box. Or if you prefer, you can do these same steps from the Open File dialog box, which you access by choosing File⇨Open.

2. From the Look In drop-down list, select Add/Modify FTP locations. Doing so brings up the Add/Modify FTP Locations dialog box.

3. In the Name of FTP site text box, enter the name of the FTP site. For example, for the Dummies FTP site, you would type **ftp.dummies.com**.

4. In the Log On As area, choose how you want to log on to the FTP site. If you want to log on anonymously, select the Anonymous radio button. If you're a registered user, select the User radio button and then type your name in the text box to the right of that button.

5. Type your password in the Password text box.

When you log on anonymously, most FTP sites either request or require that you use your e-mail address as your logon password.

6. Click the Add button to add your FTP location to the FTP sites area. You can also edit a location by clicking it in the FTP sites area and then clicking the Modify button. Similarly, you can delete a location by selecting it and clicking the Delete button.

7. Click OK in the Add/Modify FTP Locations dialog box to activate the connection and return to the Open Web dialog box.

8. Click Cancel to return to FrontPage 2000.

Publishing a Web by using FTP

People were publishing Web sites by using the Internet File Transfer Protocol long before Microsoft came along and tried to make the whole process transparent to the user. Now, with FrontPage 2000, you can finally connect to any server on the Internet by using FTP and publish your content.

There are actually two parts to the process of publishing with FTP. The first is to make your FTP connection, described in the preceding section. The second is to publish the content, which you do by following these steps:

1. Choose File⇨Publish Web from the menu bar. This brings up the Publish Web dialog box.

2. Click the Browse button to access the Open Web dialog box.

3. From the Look In drop-down list, select an FTP location from beneath the Add/Modify FTP Location indicator. The site you select appears in the Folder Name text box at the bottom of the dialog box.

4. Click Open to return to the Publish Web dialog box. You see that your FTP location has been entered in the Specify the Location to Publish Your Web To field.

5. Click the Publish button to FTP your content to the server.

Connecting to a FrontPage server

Here's a simple example to illustrate how the FrontPage server concept works. Say you're working remotely on a Web site. You've been assigned a laptop that has FrontPage 2000 on it but does not have the site on it. The Web site is being hosted on a FrontPage server back at your corporate office. With FrontPage 2000 on the laptop, you can remotely connect to the site, as if you were working locally on it, and make changes to the site in real time without ever having to click the Publish button.

Here's yet another friendly plug to go get *FrontPage 2000 For Dummies.* It has more information on FrontPage servers and how you use, configure, and access them.

Here's how to connect to a FrontPage server:

1. From the menu bar, choose File➪Open Web to bring up the Open Web dialog box.

2. Click the Web Folders button in the series of buttons along the left-hand side of the dialog box. You can also select it from the Look In drop-down list.

3. In the Folder Name text box, enter the name of the FrontPage server to which you want to connect.

4. Click the Open button to connect to the FrontPage server. FrontPage prompts you for a user name and password when you try to connect. After you enter these, the program displays the parts of the Web to which you have access.

If you aren't connected to the Internet when you try to connect to a FrontPage server, FrontPage 2000 tells you that the FrontPage 2000 server extensions could not be loaded. Though accurate, this message is a bit misleading, so be sure to double-check that connection before you log on.

Recalculating a Project's Hyperlinks

Through the process of building pages, moving folders around, and generally doing the work that's required in maintaining a Web site, some things are liable get broken. Hyperlinks are usually the first things to go. To combat this, FrontPage 2000 includes the Hyperlinks View, which enables you to see the links to and from every page and graphic on your site.

Ah, but if it's broken and you can't see it amid the links, how do you know that it's broken? That's where FrontPage's Recalculate Hyperlinks feature comes in handy. This feature performs the following tasks:

✦ Repairs all the broken hyperlinks in your Web. If hyperlinks require the use of this feature, repair means reconciling old, out-of-date link locations with up-to-date ones.

✦ Updates the rest of FrontPage so that the program knows that you made changes to your Web site. This feature is especially useful in using features such as Shared Borders, which can affect multiple pages. (*See* "Assigning Shared Borders to Pages," earlier in this part, for more information about Shared Borders.)

✦ Synchronizes any database tables that may use the new link information.

To recalculate hyperlinks, choose Tools➪Recalculate Hyperlinks. FrontPage warns you that recalculating may take a while and asks whether you really want to do it. Select Yes when prompted, and you're off. Although a progress indicator doesn't appear, the bottom-left corner shows you that FrontPage is recalculating your hyperlinks.

Resizing View Windows

Just because Microsoft sets the default window size for every view doesn't mean that you need to keep it that way. You have options for resizing your view windows, including the following:

✦ **Closing all your other windows:** Having a multitude of windows open can clutter your screen and make it difficult to view the Web pages that you're working on. Closing windows, though an extreme method of resizing, can give you more space. The Views Bar always defaults to on. If it's on, you can turn it off by choosing View➪Views Bar. If the Folder List is open, you can close that in similar fashion by choosing View➪Folder List.

✦ **Fiddling with the window width:** You can vertically resize every floating window (for example, the Folder List or the View Bar) that's open on-screen in order to gain (or lose) screen real estate. Here's how you do it:

  1. Move the mouse pointer over the right edge of a window until the mouse cursor changes from an arrow to a bar with arrows pointing in either direction.

  2. Click and hold down the mouse button.

  3. Drag the edge right or left to increase or decrease the size of the floating window and, as a result, increase or decrease the size of the Views window.

Resource Allocation in FrontPage 2000

In FrontPage 2000, there's a distinction between users who have permission to do something — say, to access the Web — and resources that are assigned ownership of an object or are assigned to accomplish a task. The former is controlled by the Web's permissions (covered in "Setting Permissions," later in this part). The latter is controlled by the administrator (that is, you, more than likely) of the Web, and is used to facilitate the process of moving Web page creation, graphics development, and even script development through the production processes of design, creation, approval, and then publishing.

Although you might think that permissions and task/object assignment would be handled identically, this separation proves to be quite useful when, for example, you have an external resource such as a copywriter working on your Web. A copywriter could be responsible for creating the words of your site, but there's a good chance that he or she would never need to get into FrontPage. Adding permissions for a user who never accesses the Web would serve no purpose! Still, you want to track the user's progress. Separating tasks and object assignment from permissions is the best way to do so.

You can add resources to a Web only if you have administration privileges. For more information about related permissions, check out "Setting Permissions" later in this part.

To add a resource to your Web, follow these steps:

1. Right-click any HTML page or graphics file in the Folders View and then choose Properties from the pop-up menu. This activates the Properties dialog box for that object.

2. Select the Workgroup tab of the Properties dialog box.

3. Click the Names button to open the Usernames Master List dialog box, as shown in the following figure.

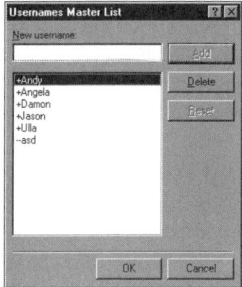

4. In the New Username field, type the name of the resource you want to add.

5. Click the Add button to add the new status to the Usernames Master List.

6. Click OK to return to the Properties dialog box.

7. Click OK or Cancel to close the Properties dialog box.

After you complete these steps, you can assign a task or ownership of an object to a resource in a couple of ways. I describe them in the following sections.

Assigning ownership of an object

In FrontPage 2000, an object can be an HTML page, a graphic, a media file (such as a sound), or even an applet. To assign ownership of an object, follow these steps:

1. Right-click the object to which you want to assign ownership and then choose Properties from the pop-up menu. This brings up the Properties dialog box specific to that object.

2. Select the Workgroup tab of the Properties dialog box.

3. In the Assigned To drop-down list, select the name that you want to assign to an object.

4. Click OK to assign the name to the object that you selected.

Assigning ownership of a task

There are a number of ways to create a task, as explained in "Creating Tasks" earlier in this part. When you create a new task, you bring up the New Task dialog box. There, you can assign a resource to a task by selecting a name from the Assigned To drop-down list. The resources that are available to assign to a task are the ones previously defined in the Workgroup tab. (*See also* "Resource Allocation in FrontPage 2000," earlier in this part.)

Another way to view the task list as a whole is through the Task View. Here, you can change the assignment of resources to a task. First switch to the Task View by choosing View⇨Tasks from the menu bar. Click the Assigned To field for a given task. A drop-down list appears. From that list, you can select a new resource to be assigned to the task.

Setting Permissions

If you're working on a Web site by yourself on your local machine, you probably don't need to know much about permissions.

However, if, say, you're managing the production process for a Web site that 20 employees and 10 contractors from various locations inside and outside your company are working on, that's a different story!

For any Web, FrontPage comes with three basic security and permission options:

✦ **Browse This Web:** This security level enables users to log on to a Web and look at all the pages, but they can't change any of the files.

✦ **Author and Browse This Web:** This security level lets users both browse a Web and add, delete, and edit existing Web files.

✦ **Administer, Author, and Browse This Web:** With this, the highest level of access, users can browse and author within a Web, as well as give access privileges to other users and change their own access privileges.

You can access FrontPage 2000's security settings by choosing Tools⇨Security⇨Permissions from the menu bar. That said, you may find that you don't even have the ability to use FrontPage's security features. You'll know that this is the case if you try to choose Security but can't because it's grayed out.

You can use FrontPage 2000's security features and add new users to a FrontPage 2000 Web only if

✦ Your Web is being hosted on a FrontPage server.

   OR

✦ Your local machine is working as a FrontPage server (this requires an NTFS-formatted hard drive) and the Web is on your local machine.

   AND

✦ You are registered as the administrator for the Web, or the administrator has granted you administration privileges for the Web.

With FrontPage 2000, the breadth and type of permission handling you have access to are based on the kind of FrontPage server on which your Web is being hosted. Essentially, there are two types of Web servers: those that run on UNIX and those that run on Windows NT. Far and away, Apache is the most popular UNIX server (there's also an NT version), and Microsoft Internet Information Services (IIS) is the most popular Windows NT server. You can check which kind of server your Web is being hosted on by choosing Tools⇨Web Settings from the menu bar. Next to the Server Version label is the server and version number that your Web is being hosted on.

Setting permissions on a Microsoft IIS server

An increasingly large number of Microsoft servers out on the Internet are being used for Web hosting. As you might expect, they're fully optimized to support FrontPage servers.

When you use Windows NT and IIS, you inherit users and their initial permission status from the Windows NT server list of users. As the administrator of a Web on this server, you can add, remove, and edit the privileges of users who have already been created in the Windows NT server by the server administrator. You cannot, however, create new users — or delete users, for that matter — to be added to the Windows NT server list.

Knowing how Windows NT server works is integral to using the multi-user components of FrontPage. I highly recommend grabbing a copy of *Windows NT Networking For Dummies* by Ed Tittel, Mary Madden, and Earl Follis (published by IDG Books Worldwide, Inc.) to get a more complete picture of how Windows NT Server works.

The first thing you need to decide when using the Windows NT server for setting permissions is whether you want to have the permissions of the parent Web (in this case, the parent Web is the folder on the Windows NT server computer that uses the FrontPage server extensions) or whether you want your Web to have its own permissions.

To set your desired permissions settings, follow these steps:

1. Choose Tools⊅Security⊅Permissions from the menu bar to bring up the Permissions dialog box. The Settings tab should be the default tab that appears. If it isn't, select the Settings tab.

2. Select one of the two available radio buttons (shown in the following figure) to set the proper permissions. You're probably going to want a unique set of permissions for your Web. If this is the case, select Use Unique Permissions for This Web. If your MIS administrator has set the permissions for the FrontPage server the way you need them, however, select Use Same Permissions as Parent Web.

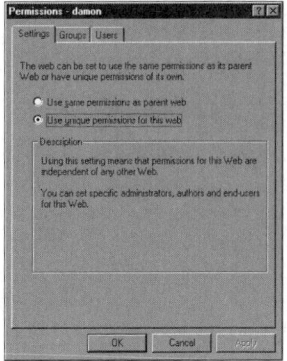

3. Click the Apply button to apply the changes to your Web.

If you choose to inherit the permissions of the parent Web, you can't add or edit the profiles of any users or groups in the other tabs of the Permissions dialog box. If you're creating unique permissions for your own Web, however, you can add users and groups by following these steps:

1. Choose Tools➪Security➪Permissions from the menu bar. This brings up the Permissions dialog box.

2. To edit a user, select the Users tab. The view changes, as shown in the following figure.

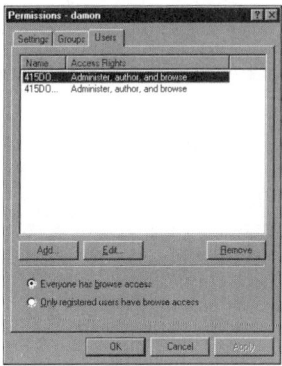

3. Click the Add button to bring up the Add Users dialog box, as shown in the following figure. Along the left-hand side of the dialog box is a Names list, which includes all the active users on the NT server domain. If you have more than one domain to choose from, you can select the one that you want in the Obtain List From drop-down list.

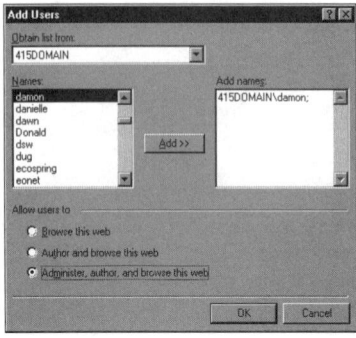

4. Click the name that you want to add and then click the Add button. Doing so adds the name you've chosen to the Add Names list along the right side of the dialog box.

5. Set the permissions for the users in the Add Names list by choosing one of the three security options in the Allow Users To area of the Add Users dialog box.

When you set permissions by using this method, FrontPage applies the permission level to all the users in the Add Names list. You can't assign permission access to individual users from this dialog box. You can, however, add all the browse-level users first, all the author-level users second, and so on.

6. Click OK to add this group of users to the Users tab in the Permissions dialog box.

Adding groups works exactly the same way. To add group permissions, just click the Group tab of the Permissions dialog box and then follow the preceding steps.

If you want to edit a user's access privileges after you've added the user, click the user's name on the Users tab of the Permissions dialog box and then click the Edit button. You get the Edit Users dialog box. From there, you can change a user's access by selecting one of the three radio buttons (as shown in the following figure) and then clicking OK.

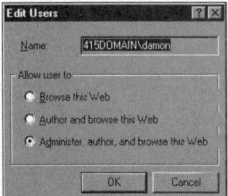

Setting permissions on a UNIX server

Note: The following steps assume that Apache is being used as the Web server software on UNIX machines. Other Web server software may offer variations to the features that Apache supports.

One of the problems with explaining permissions in FrontPage is that it's fundamentally different, depending on what kind of server you're working on. One thing is for sure, though: If your Web resides on a UNIX computer, there's a pretty good chance that the UNIX computer is using Apache for the Web server software.

If that's the case, follow these steps to grant a new user access to a Web:

1. Choose Tools➪Security➪Permissions from the menu bar. This brings up the Permissions dialog box.

You can set your Web so that everyone who opens it in FrontPage 2000 or views it with a browser is able to browse the files. Just select the Everyone Has Browse Access radio button in the Permissions dialog box and click OK to enable this feature. Alternatively, if you want to restrict access to only registered users, click the Only Registered Users Have Browse Access button.

2. Click the Add button. This brings up the Add Users dialog box, as shown in the following figure.

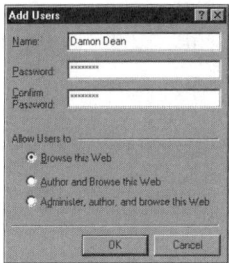

3. Type the user's name and password, respectively, in the Name and Password text boxes. Confirm the password by re-entering it in the Confirm Password box.

4. Select the access level for the new user by choosing one of the three security options in the Allow Users To area of the Add Users dialog box.

5. Click OK to add the user to the Permissions dialog box.

6. Click OK in the Permissions dialog box to enable the new user's access privileges in FrontPage 2000.

You may want to be able to grant access not by user name but by computer name. The most recognizable and secure way to do so is to use a computer's Internet Protocol (IP) address. Setting permissions by using an IP address works essentially the same as it does for setting permissions by user name and password.

Here's how you do it:

1. From the menu bar, choose Tools⇨Security⇨Permissions. This brings up the Permissions dialog box.

2. Select the Computers tab to switch to the current permissions attached to IP addresses.

3. Click the Add button to bring up the Add Computer dialog box, as shown in the following figure.

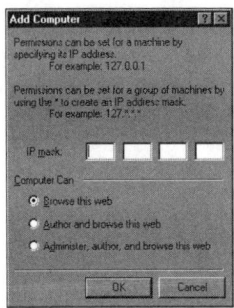

4. In the IP Mask field, type the TCP/IP address of the computer to which you want to give permission.

5. Select the access level for the new user by choosing one of the three security options in the Computer Can area of the Add Computer dialog box.

6. Click OK to add the computer to the Permissions dialog box.

7. Click OK in the Permissions dialog box to enable the new computer access privileges in FrontPage 2000.

Testing Your Network Settings

If you're having trouble posting content to the Internet, you may want to double-check your network settings to make sure that your connection is up and running correctly. To test your network settings, follow these steps:

1. Choose Help⇨About Microsoft FrontPage from the menu bar. The About Microsoft FrontPage dialog box appears, as shown in the following figure. (I know, I know — it's a weird place for this feature.)

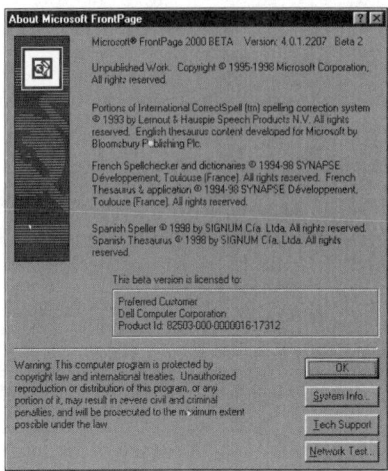

2. Click the Network Test button to open the FrontPage TCP/IP Test dialog box, which includes diagnostic tests for Winsock, plus retrieval of vital information such as your TCP/IP address and your host name.

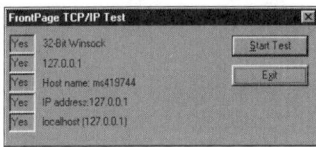

3. Click Start Test to run the test.

If the test is successful, you see a series of yeses in the dialog box. If you get some nos, your Internet connection probably isn't configured correctly.

For more information about setting up an Internet connection, see *The Internet For Dummies,* 5th Edition, by John R. Levine, Carol Baroudi, and Margy Levine Young (published by IDG Books Worldwide, Inc.).

Toolbar Customization

Now that FrontPage 2000 is included in the Microsoft Office suite, it comes with the requisite Office toolbars, including the Standard and Formatting Toolbars. In addition to these two toolbars, FrontPage supports seven other toolbars that you can display and customize.

The following table highlights the functions of each toolbar.

Toolbar	Features
Standard	Includes such general Office functions as Open, Save, and Print.
Formatting	Provides font-style and formatting functions.
DHTML Effects	Assigns Dynamic HTML events to things like mouse clicks and rollovers. (**See** Part VII for more information about using Dynamic HTML.)
Navigation	Lets you control the layout and size of the Navigation View. You can also use this toolbar to add external links.
Picture	Gives you point-and-click access to all the image-editing tools built into FrontPage 2000.
Positioning	Enables you to set locations and move the position of objects on a page.
Reports	Makes all the FrontPage reports accessible through a drop-down list.
Style	Launches the Cascading Style Sheet dialog box.
Table	Generates quick and easy HTML tables.

Adding and removing toolbars

To display a toolbar, choose View⇨Toolbars⇨*Name_of_the_toolbar*. After you choose the toolbar you want, a recessed check mark appears in the menu next to the name of the toolbar, and the toolbar you chose will either float on-screen or sit next to the Standard and Formatting Toolbars.

If a toolbar appears to be floating randomly on-screen, you can drag it up to the location of the other toolbars. After you get the toolbar up there, the toolbar area grows to accommodate the new toolbar. You can also double-click the title bar of a floating toolbar to mount it with the other nonfloating toolbars.

Customizing toolbars

In addition to selecting from the preset toolbars, FrontPage enables you to customize the toolbars to your liking through the Customize dialog box, as shown in the following figure.

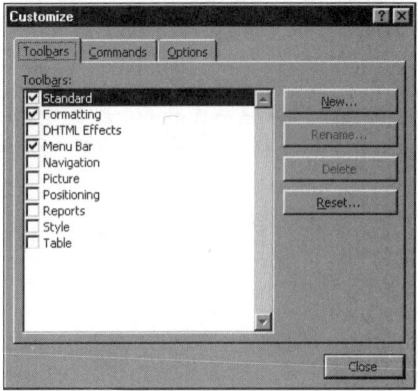

Choose Vieweee⇒Toolbarseee⇒Customize to open the Customize dialog box. In the Customize dialog box, you find three areas in which you can make changes to the toolbars. The following list describes each area:

✦ **Toolbars tab:** The Toolbars tab provides another way of selecting any of the preset toolbars. The only difference between using this method and using the menu bar is that here you can add or subtract more than one toolbar at a time. You can also create your own custom toolbars in this tab.

✦ **Commands tab:** The Commands tab offers a handy way to modify the existing toolbars to fit your preferences. This tab is split into two sections:

  • *Categories* lists all the FrontPage file menus, plus a category for macros.

  • *Commands* are the features available in those categories. If you want to know what a particular command does, click the command and then click the Description button. To customize a toolbar, drag an icon from the Command section onto the toolbar . . . and bingo! That command is now available on that toolbar, icon and all.

  Remember: You can place an icon anywhere on a toolbar — just drag the icon to the location of your choosing. If a vertical bar appears to the right of where you want the icon to go, you know that the icon will land in the correct place. After you release the mouse button, the new icon appears directly to the left of the bar.

✦ **Options tab:** The Options tab lets you specify a number of options for your toolbars, including icon size, toolbar placement, and even animations, which enable your pull-down menus to scroll down or reveal out when clicked.

Viewing a Web Object's Properties

Every object within your Web has a series of properties associated with it. You can set these properties in the object's Properties dialog box. To access the Properties dialog box, follow these steps:

1. Find the object for which you want to view properties.

2. Right-click the object and choose Properties from the pop-up menu. The Properties dialog box for that object appears, as shown in the following figure.

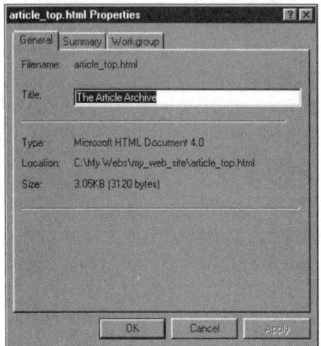

3. Edit the object's properties. Three tabs on the dialog box enable you to change the following items:

• **Title of the Object:** FrontPage defaults to the General tab. This tab provides one of the many ways in which you can rename an object in FrontPage 2000. To rename an object, insert a new name in the Title field.

Renaming an object doesn't change the name of the actual file but rather changes the name associated with the file. In the case of an HTML page, this name is that of the page that the header specifies. For a graphics image, the name's just a line of text that FrontPage uses to identify that object.

• **Text in the Comment text box:** Sometimes, you need to leave notes about a page or an object. Select the Summary tab, and you can enter text in the Comment text box that will be saved for others to review.

• **Workgroup tab:** On the Workgroup tab, you can categorize the object, assign review status to the object, and assign resources to work on the object. (*See* Part VII for more information about the Workgroup tab and all the features it entails.)

4. After you complete your edits, click OK to exit the Properties dialog box and implement the changes to the object.

Working with the Hyperlinks View

One of the nice things about the Hyperlinks View is that you can choose any object in your Web site — including HTML pages and graphics — and see exactly what pages or other objects are linked into that object. You can also see where the object links. With the Folder List open, all you have to do is click an object, and the Hyperlinks View displays all the links to and from that page, as shown in the following figure.

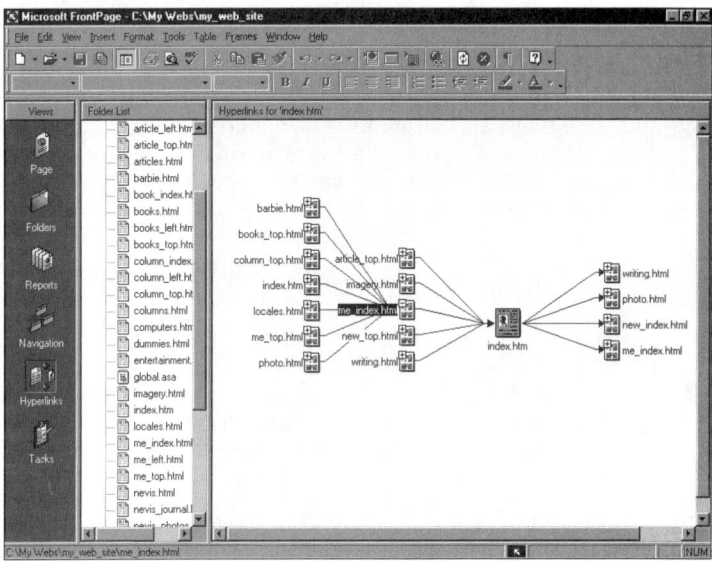

The options that you can specify while working in the Hyperlinks View include the following:

✦ **Move to Center:** Say you're looking at a file with a few pages linked to it. The file you've chosen is in the middle, and the linked pages are on either side of it. Now suppose that you want to see the link structure of one of those other pages that's linked to the page you're currently reviewing. Just right-click that page in the Hyperlinks View window and choose Move to Center from the pop-up menu. Bingo! That page is now the middle page, and it shows all the links to and from it.

 ✦ **Hyperlinks to Pictures:** To see the links to images in your Web site from the Hyperlinks View window, right-click an open area in the Hyperlinks View window and then choose Hyperlinks to Pictures from the pop-up menu.

 ✦ **Show Page Titles:** Do you remember page titles better than you do HTML page names? If so, from the Hyperlinks View window, right-click an open area and choose Show Page Titles from the pop-up menu to view your hyperlinks by their page titles.

 ✦ **Repeated Hyperlinks:** Want to see whether some of your links are being duplicated? From the Hyperlinks View window, right-click an open area and choose Repeated Hyperlinks from the pop-up menu.

Working with Reports

FrontPage 2000 provides 14 useful reports that give you a better idea of what's going right — and what's going wrong — with your Web site. The reports cover all the major areas of a Web site, including file summaries, links reports, publishing status, and version control checking. Unlike other elements of FrontPage, these reports aren't particularly customizable. On the upside, however, you can easily access and generate the reports.

To generate a report, choose View➪Reports. FrontPage 2000 generates a site summary report for you, which includes information in 15 different categories. To view a more detailed report based on one of these categories, double-click the name of the report you want to view. FrontPage compiles the report and displays the results for you in the Reports View.

In all the reports that FrontPage creates, you can double-click a file, and FrontPage launches the Associated Editor for that file type.

Site Summary report

A *Site Summary* report takes various pieces of data from each of the 13 other reports and distills it down to one line to provide you with a quick picture of what's going on in your Web site. This report includes the following items:

 ✦ A total count of all the files on your Web

 ✦ A total count of all the images on your Web

 ✦ The number of linked and unlinked files on your Web

 ✦ The number of broken links — both internal and external — to your Web

✦ The number of component errors on your Web (*see* Part VII for information about using FrontPage 2000 components in your Web)

✦ The number of current tasks that remain uncompleted on your Web

✦ The slow pages on your Web

✦ A listing of both the newly added pages and the older pages on your Web

✦ The currently unused but active themes for that Web (*see* "Applying a New Theme to a Web," earlier in this part, for more information about using themes in FrontPage 2000)

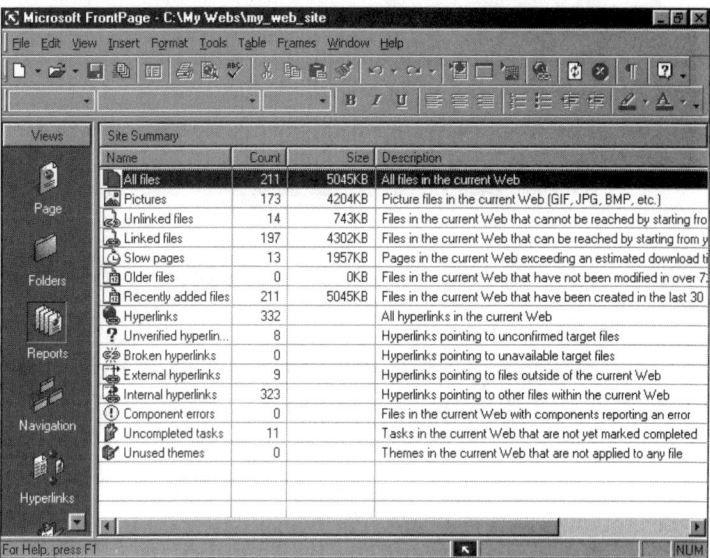

All Files report

Believe it or not, the All Files report sounds surprisingly similar to what it is. This handy grid report gives you nine fields worth of data for every single file in your Web. The All Files report includes the following information:

✦ Filename

✦ File title

✦ The file's folder location

✦ Whether the file is an "orphan" (a file that you can't reach by following hyperlinks from your home page)

+ File size

+ File type

+ The last day someone modified the file

+ The last person to modify the file

+ A comment field for you to input notes about a file

Name	Title	In Folder	Size	Type	Modi
ad.gif	ad.gif		2KB	gif	2/8/9
advice.gif	images/advice.gif	images	19KB	gif	2/8/9
advice.jpg	images/advice.jpg	images	137KB	jpg	2/8/9
aids.gif	images/aids.gif	images	20KB	gif	2/8/9
aids.jpg	images/aids.jpg	images	142KB	jpg	2/8/9
arrow.gif	images/arrow.gif	images	1KB	gif	2/8/9
artbgrd_left.gif	images/artbgrd_left.gif	images	6KB	gif	2/8/9
artbgrd_top.gif	images/artbgrd_top.gif	images	5KB	gif	2/8/9
article_head.gif	images/article_head.gif	images	1KB	gif	2/8/9
article_index.h...	The Article Archive		1KB	html	2/8/9
article_left.html	The Article Archive		1KB	html	2/8/9
article_top.html	The Article Archive		3KB	html	2/8/9
articles.html	The Article Archive		4KB	html	2/8/9
bar.GIF	images/bar.GIF	images	11KB	GIF	2/8/9
barbie1.gif	images/barbie1.gif	images	28KB	gif	2/8/9
barbie2_big.gif	images/barbie2_big.gif	images	132KB	gif	2/8/9

To sort the report data, click the header of one of the grid columns. Click the same header a second time, and FrontPage sorts the report data in the opposite order.

Recently Added, Recently Changed, and Older File reports

The Recently Added, Recently Changed, and Older File reports all look similar to one another and to the All Files report. In fact, the only difference between these three reports and the All Files report is that the former lack the Comment and Orphan fields. In short, these reports tell you what you've added to your Web, what you've changed within your Web, and what your Web has contained for a while.

The value of these reports lies in keeping track of how often you change your data, as indicated in the Modified Date field, shown in the following figure. If the data in your site changes constantly, these reports can help you troubleshoot problems in your site that relate to changes that occur at or around a certain time. These reports can also tell you when to remove pages, hyperlinks, or graphics from your site because they're not being used or accessed.

Name	Title	Created Date	Modified By	Size	T
invoices.mdb	databases/invoices.mdb	2/9/99 9:17 PM	Damon Dean	348KB	m
global.asa	global.asa	2/9/99 9:17 PM	Damon Dean	2KB	a
clients.mdb	databases/clients.mdb	2/9/99 9:17 PM	Damon Dean	348KB	m
new_page_2...	new_page_2.htm	2/9/99 12:31 AM	Damon Dean	1KB	h
index.htm	Welcome To Damon's Lou...	2/8/99 10:40 PM	Damon Dean	7KB	h
courtyard.GIF	images/courtyard.GIF	2/8/99 10:36 PM	Damon Dean	8KB	G
dining.GIF	images/dining.GIF	2/8/99 10:36 PM	Damon Dean	12KB	G
library.GIF	images/library.GIF	2/8/99 10:36 PM	Damon Dean	9KB	G
bar.GIF	images/bar.GIF	2/8/99 10:36 PM	Damon Dean	11KB	G
charleston.GIF	images/charleston.GIF	2/8/99 10:36 PM	Damon Dean	10KB	G
hamilton.GIF	images/hamilton.GIF	2/8/99 10:36 PM	Damon Dean	12KB	G
ruins1.GIF	images/ruins1.GIF	2/8/99 10:36 PM	Damon Dean	8KB	G
oualie1.GIF	images/oualie1.GIF	2/8/99 10:36 PM	Damon Dean	12KB	G
stkitts.GIF	images/stkitts.GIF	2/8/99 10:36 PM	Damon Dean	7KB	G
monkey2.GIF	images/monkey2.GIF	2/8/99 10:35 PM	Damon Dean	13KB	G
hike1.GIF	images/hike1.GIF	2/8/99 10:35 PM	Damon Dean	10KB	G
hike2.GIF	images/hike2.GIF	2/8/99 10:35 PM	Damon Dean	12KB	G

Follow these steps to define both "recent" and "older" Web data:

1. Choose Tools⇨Options to activate the FrontPage Options dialog box.

2. Click the Reports View tab.

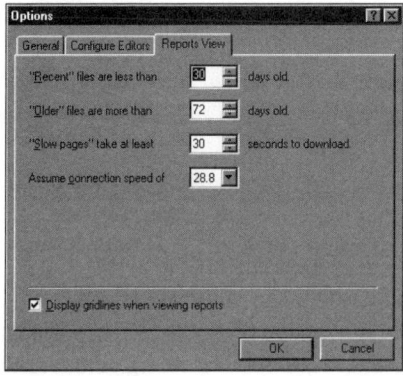

3. Set your preferences for Recent and Older files by inputting a number in the "Recent" Files Are Less Than and "Older" Files Are More Than fields.

4. Click OK to activate your new settings. FrontPage recalculates the report and displays the updated results for you.

Hyperlink reports

FrontPage 2000 includes two hyperlink reports, the Unlinked Files report and the Broken Hyperlinks report (shown in the following figure). The Unlinked Files report is often quite large because it commonly includes a number of graphics on your Web site that don't link to anything. You can use this report to make sure that no errant HTML files show up accidentally in your Web.

Status	Hyperlink	In Page	Page Title
Broken Hyperlinks			
? Unknown	http://ad.doubleclick.net/ad/www.mi...	pocket.html	404 Error Page
? Unknown	http://ad.doubleclick.net/jump/www...	pocket.html	404 Error Page
? Unknown	http://www.amazon.com	dummies.html	The Book Archive
? Unknown	http://www.dummies.com	books.html	The Book Archive
? Unknown	http://www.idgbooks.com	books.html	The Book Archive
? Unknown	http://www.mindspring.com/	pocket.html	404 Error Page
? Unknown	http://www.mindspring.com/ad.html	pocket.html	404 Error Page
? Unknown	http://www.sybex.com	books.html	The Book Archive

The Broken Hyperlinks report is a much more useful tool than the Unlinked Files report because it tells you about the hyperlinks on your Web site that don't go to an active location or that FrontPage can't verify. The Unlinked Files Report, in contrast, simply tells you which files don't have links.

When you're in the Broken Hyperlinks report, you can click a broken or unknown link, and the Edit Hyperlink dialog box appears.

If FrontPage 2000 can't verify a link, it's usually because you're not connected to the Internet when the report is being generated. During the report-generation process, FrontPage checks the destination of all outbound links to make sure that they get a return signal from the server. If FrontPage can't make a connection to check the validity of the link, it simply tells you that it can't verify the hyperlink.

You can perform the following functions in the Edit Hyperlink dialog box:

+ Jump to the HTML page to find the broken hyperlink.

+ Input a new link in the Replace Hyperlink With text box to manually update the hyperlink.

+ Click the Browse button to replace the broken hyperlink within your Web.

+ Fix the broken hyperlink in all the pages on which it appears, or only in specific pages.

Note: If you don't have a connection to the Internet and your links point to other Web sites, FrontPage lists those links as Unknown on the Broken Hyperlinks report.

Slow Pages report

The Slow Pages report is perhaps the most valuable of the FrontPage 2000 reports simply because it gives you critical information about the one thing that users hate: slow-loading pages. FrontPage looks at a number of factors to determine whether a page loads quickly or slowly, including the number of graphics, frames, scripts, and applets it contains.

After FrontPage finishes profiling these factors, it generates a report of the slowest pages and their estimated download time. Of course, download time is relative to connection speed, but FrontPage enables you to set the parameters for what constitutes a slow page.

Slow Pages					
Name	Title	Download Time	Size	Type	In Folder
trade.html	Computer Game Articles	99 Seconds	5KB	html	
locales.html	The Locales Archive	67 Seconds	6KB	html	
column_index....	The Column Archive	85 Seconds	1KB	html	
writing.html	Something From The Library?	33 Seconds	6KB	html	
index.htm	Welcome To Damon's Lou...	145 Seconds	7KB	htm	
computers.html	Computer Game Articles	135 Seconds	6KB	html	
entertainment....	The Entertainment Titles	34 Seconds	2KB	html	
book_index.html	The Book Archive	38 Seconds	1KB	html	
nevis_photos....	The Locales Archive	80 Seconds	4KB	html	
me_index.html	What About Damon?	152 Seconds	1KB	html	
imagery.html	The Imagery Archive	52 Seconds	5KB	html	
columns.html	The Columns Archive	76 Seconds	6KB	html	
photo.html	You Call That Photography?	42 Seconds	6KB	html	

Follow these steps to change your Slow Pages report preferences:

1. Choose Tools⇨Options to activate the FrontPage Options dialog box.

2. Select the Reports View tab.

3. Set your time preferences for Slow Pages and the target modem speed for calculating download time. You set these two options by typing a time (in seconds) in the "Slow Pages" Take at Least field and then choosing a default connection from the Assume Connection Speed Of drop-down list.

4. Click OK to activate your new settings. FrontPage recalculates the report and displays the updated results.

Note: In the Slow Pages report, FrontPage provides a Size field. This field is somewhat misleading. The Size field refers to the Web page itself, which is often small. The field doesn't, however, include all the graphics associated with that file.

Component Error reports

FrontPage 2000 includes 15 different component categories. A lot
can go wrong with components if you're not careful. Luckily,
FrontPage provides a report that checks out the functionality of
components such as banners and forms, as well as scheduled
items such as pictures.

Although the report tells you about your components' problems, it
doesn't do much to help you fix the problems that it finds. The
Component Error report gives you a lengthy explanation of what
went wrong, but unlike the Broken Hyperlinks report, it doesn't
provide a dialog box to enable you to fix problems that may arise.
You can, however, double-click the individual error, and FrontPage
transports you to the location in the Normal View where the problem
occurs. There, you can try to figure out the problem and fix it.

Review Status and Assigned To reports

The Review Status and Assigned To reports are for managers who
control Web production and publishing processes in multi-user
environments. These reports quickly provide you with basic file
information, information about where a file currently resides in the
production flow, and information about who reviews the file in
the production flow.

See also "Assigning Review Status to an Object" and "Resource
Allocation in FrontPage 2000," both earlier in this part.

Unlike the other reports in FrontPage, which generally provide you
with Web site information that you can view only, the Review
Status report includes fields that you can actually edit right from
the report itself. You can quickly and easily change the production
status of files and reallocate the resources that those files task.

Name	Title	Review Status	Assigned To	Review Dat
trade.html	Computer Game Articles	Code Review		2/5/37 10:2
new_page_2...	new_page_2.htm	Content Review		2/5/37 10:2
sf3_big.gif	images/sf3_big.gif	Legal Review		2/5/37 10:2
ny4_big.gif	images/ny4_big.gif			
nevis_damon.gif	images/nevis_damon.gif			
monkey3.GIF	images/monkey3.GIF			
executions.GIF	images/executions.GIF			
dc3_big.gif	images/dc3_big.gif			
books_left.html	The Books Archive	Content Review		
articles.html	The Article Archive	Code Review		
article_top.html	The Article Archive	Content Review		
photo_billboar...	images/photo_billboard.gif	Legal Review / Manager Review		
ib_293.GIF	images/ib_293.GIF			
colbgrd_left.gif	images/colbgrd_left.gif			
bokbgrd_top.gif	images/bokbgrd_top.gif			
barbie3_sml.gif	images/barbie3_sml.gif			
advice.jpg	images/advice.jpg			

The only downside to using the Review Status report is that you get information about all the files in the Web site. FrontPage provides no way for you to customize the report to view it only by review status, assignment, or review date.

Category and Checkout Status reports

Next to the All Files report, the Category report is perhaps the simplest FrontPage 2000 report, both in terms of use and in terms of the information it provides. This report sorts your pages and images by the categories that you assign to them.

Categories

Name	Title	Category	Type	In Folder	
artbgrd_left.gif	images/artbgrd_left.gif	Goals/Objectives	gif	images	
artbgrd_top.gif	images/artbgrd_top.gif	Expense Report	gif	images	
article_head.gif	images/article_head.gif	Expense Report	gif	images	
article_index.h...	The Article Archive	Expense Report	html		
article_left.html	The Article Archive	Expense Report	html		
article_top.html	The Article Archive	Expense Report	html		
articles.html	The Article Archive	Expense Report	html		
bar.GIF	images/bar.GIF	Expense Report	GIF	images	
advice.gif	images/advice.gif	Competition	gif	images	
ad.gif	ad.gif	Business	gif		
barbie2_sml.gif	images/barbie2_sml.gif		gif	images	
barbie3_big.gif	images/barbie3_big.gif		gif	images	
barbie3_sml.gif	images/barbie3_sml.gif		gif	images	
barbie4_big.gif	images/barbie4_big.gif		gif	images	
barbie4_sml.gif	images/barbie4_sml.gif		gif	images	
barbie5_big.gif	images/barbie5_big.gif		gif	images	
barbie5_sml.gif	images/barbie5_sml.gif		gif	images	

The Checkout Status report performs essentially the same tasks as the Category report except that the Checkout Status report includes information about who's checked out the file, the version number of the currently associated file, and the last date on which anyone committed and locked the file.

Checkout Status

	Name	Title	Checked Out By	Version	Locked Date	T
✓	article_top.h...	The Article Archive	Damon Dean	V1	2/9/99 11:00 PM	h
✓	article_left.h...	The Article Archive	Damon Dean	V1	2/9/99 11:00 PM	h
✓	book_index....	The Book Archive	Damon Dean	V1	2/9/99 11:00 PM	h
✓	books_top.h...	The Book Archive	Damon Dean	V1	2/9/99 11:00 PM	h
✓	article_index...	The Article Archive	Damon Dean	V1	2/9/99 11:00 PM	h
✓	books.html	The Book Archive	Damon Dean	V1	2/9/99 11:00 PM	h
•	new_page_...	new_page_2.htm		V1		h
•	sf3_big.gif	images/sf3_big.gif		V1		g
•	ny4_big.gif	images/ny4_big.gif		V1		g
•	nevis_damo...	images/nevis_damon.gif		V1		g
•	monkey3.GIF	images/monkey3.GIF		V1		G
•	executions....	images/executions.GIF		V1		G
•	dc3_big.gif	images/dc3_big.gif		V1		g
•	photo_billbo...	images/photo_billboard.gif		V1		g
•	ib_293.GIF	images/ib_293.GIF		V1		G
•	colbgrd_left...	images/colbgrd_left.gif		V1		g
•	bokbgrd_to...	images/bokbgrd_top.gif		V1		g

Publish Status report

The Publish Status report tells you exactly which Web file you've scheduled for publication, as well as the current review status for that Web file. As with the three multi-user reports, you can change both the file's publishing status (from Publish to Don't Publish) and the review status from this report. Consider the Publish Status report to be the last line of defense for making sure that everything's in top shape before committing your content to your Web site.

Name	Title	Publish	Modified Date	Review Stal
✓ trade.html	Computer Game Articles	Publish	2/9/99 10:56 PM	Code Revie
• new_page_...	new_page_2.htm	Publish	2/9/99 10:56 PM	Content Rev
• sf3_big.gif	images/sf3_big.gif	Publish	2/8/99 10:30 PM	Legal Revie
• ny4_big.gif	images/ny4_big.gif	Publish	2/8/99 10:31 PM	
• nevis_damo...	images/nevis_damon.gif	Publish	2/8/99 10:23 PM	
• monkey3.GIF	images/monkey3.GIF	Publish	2/8/99 10:35 PM	
• executions....	images/executions.GIF	Publish	2/8/99 10:21 PM	
• dc3_big.gif	images/dc3_big.gif	Publish	2/8/99 10:31 PM	
✓ books_left.h...	The Books Archive	Publish	2/8/99 10:21 PM	
✓ articles.html	The Article Archive	Publish	2/9/99 10:58 PM	
✓ article_top.h...	The Article Archive	Publish	2/9/99 10:58 PM	
• photo_billbo...	images/photo_billboard.gif	Publish	2/8/99 10:18 PM	
• ib_293.GIF	images/ib_293.GIF	Publish	2/8/99 10:28 PM	
• colbgrd_left....	images/colbgrd_left.gif	Publish	2/8/99 10:21 PM	
• bokbgrd_to...	images/bokbgrd_top.gif	Publish	2/8/99 10:21 PM	
• barbie3_sml...	images/barbie3_sml.gif	Publish	2/8/99 10:23 PM	
• advice.jpg	images/advice.jpg	Publish	2/8/99 10:25 PM	

Part IV

Building Web Sites with the FrontPage Editor

This part covers the innards of the FrontPage Editor. It should get you ready to build whatever it is that you want to bring to the Internet! So, to quote a number of the '80s rap CDs I've got hanging around my apartment, "Let's . . . get . . . busy!"

In this part . . .

✓ **Exploring the three views of the FrontPage Editor**

✓ **Building Navigation bars and banners**

✓ **Manipulating text and styles in HTML pages**

✓ **Inserting forms and buttons**

✓ **Generating internal and external links**

A Quick Guide to the Three Views of the FrontPage Editor

This section may break the alphabetical order rule, but it's extremely important that you understand just how the FrontPage Editor works before you get too far into it.

Like most things in FrontPage 2000, you can make the Editor as simple or as complex as you like. The Editor is designed to appeal to HTML-editing newbies as well as to HTML masters and purists. It achieves this delicate balance between the new kids on the block and the veterans by enabling users either to use drag-and-drop tools for composing pages or to edit the HTML directly.

The FrontPage Editor is split into three basic views, which you can access by clicking one of the three tabs in the bottom-left corner of the editing window:

✦ **Normal View:** This is the default view for the Editor, and undoubtedly the way Microsoft prefers that you create your Web pages.

In the Normal View (shown in the following figure), you can create Web page elements on-screen and position them anywhere you like. As you do this, FrontPage autogenerates the necessary HTML to make the page that you've created.

The idea is that FrontPage takes HTML editing out of the HTML creation process and replaces it with menus, toolbars, wizards, and other elements that Office users are accustomed to seeing.

 FrontPage 2000 employs *pixel perfect positioning.* Sounds fancy, but essentially all it means is that you can now use FrontPage to place objects (text and graphics) on-screen down to the exact pixel. With pixel perfect positioning, the pages you view with a browser look more similar to the pages that you created in the Normal view.

 Pixel perfect positioning is not an exact science, nor is it fully supported in the older Web browsers. Generally, pixel precise layouts work better with Internet Explorer Version 4.0 (or higher) and Netscape Communicator Version 4.0 (or higher).

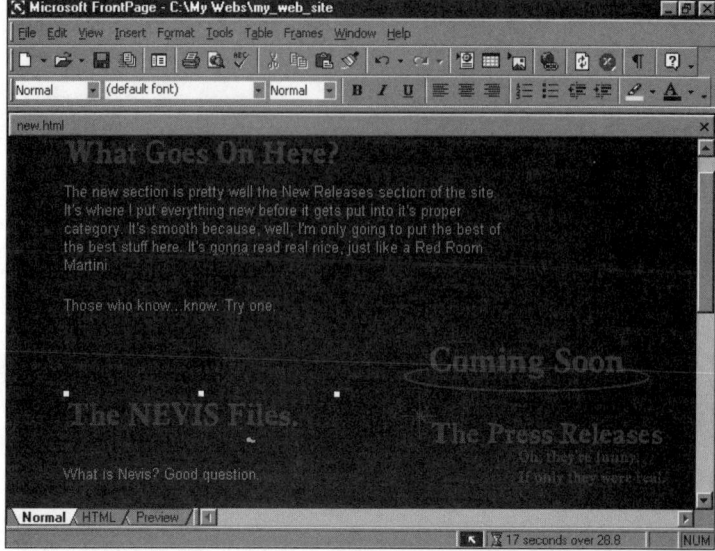

✦ **HTML View:** Prefer to do your own HTML editing? You can use the HTML View to edit your HTML directly and bypass all the automated features that the Normal View offers. This view works like a more traditional HTML editor, but it also offers a number of handy features, like HTML coloring and tag viewing, to make the editing process a little more user friendly.

In addition, you can import an existing Web page that you built in another HTML editor, and FrontPage 2000 will not change the HTML at all. That way, you can continue working on your Web page where you left off with the other HTML editor!

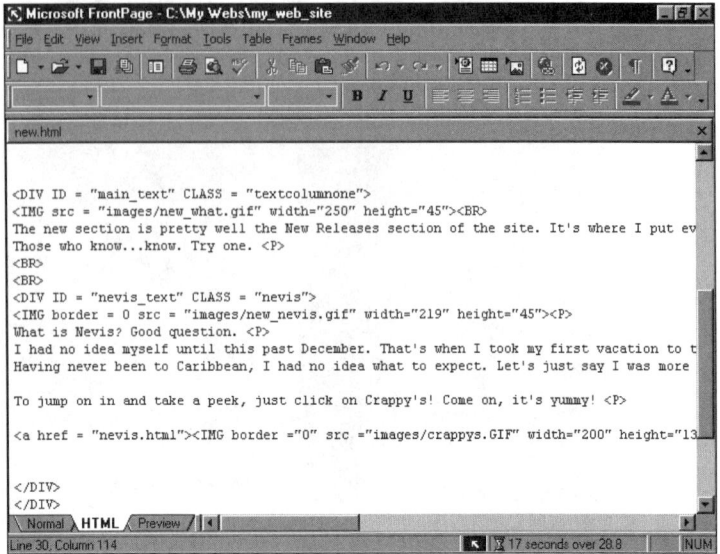

```
Microsoft FrontPage - C:\My Webs\my_web_site                           _ □ X
File  Edit  View  Insert  Format  Tools  Table  Frames  Window  Help

new.html                                                                    X

<DIV ID = "main_text" CLASS = "textcolumnone">
<IMG src = "images/new_what.gif" width="250" height="45"><BR>
The new section is pretty well the New Releases section of the site. It's where I put ev
Those who know...know. Try one. <P>
<BR>
<BR>
<DIV ID = "nevis_text" CLASS = "nevis">
<IMG border = 0 src = "images/new_nevis.gif" width="219" height="45"><P>
What is Nevis? Good question. <P>
I had no idea myself until this past December. That's when I took my first vacation to t
Having never been to Caribbean, I had no idea what to expect. Let's just say I was more

To jump on in and take a peek, just click on Crappy's! Come on, it's yummy! <P>

<a href = "nevis.html"><IMG border ="0" src ="images/crappys.GIF" width="200" height="13

</DIV>
</DIV>

Normal \ HTML / Preview / ◄

Line 30, Column 114                                    17 seconds over 28.8        NUM
```

✦ **Preview View:** The Preview View eliminates the need to open up a browser to see what your pages look like. This view, shown in the following figure, gives you an immediate idea of whether a page you've created is working properly, because Preview View works like Internet Explorer emulator.

You'd use the Preview View to, for example, see whether JavaScript and Dynamic HTML rollovers are working properly, or to see whether the queries you've made to a database are being processed correctly.

The Preview View is a good idea . . . almost. The downside is that it emulates Internet Explorer, which means that if you use the Preview View as the only method of previewing your work, you're neglecting the large number of Web users who use some form of Netscape Navigator.

See "Previewing Web Pages in a Browser" in Part III for more information about previewing your pages in a browser.

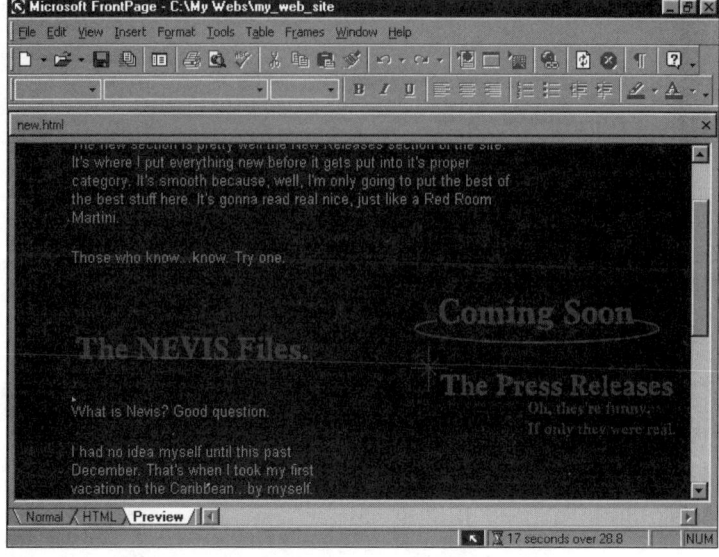

Adding Clip Art to a Web Page

FrontPage 2000 comes with an extensive Clip Art gallery that helps you easily create buttons and banners, as well as communicate all kinds of different themes and emotions. To add clip art to your Web page, follow these steps:

   1. Choose Insert⇨Picture⇨Clip. The Clip Art Gallery dialog box appears. Notice that you can add various types of clip art, including graphics, sound files, and video clips.

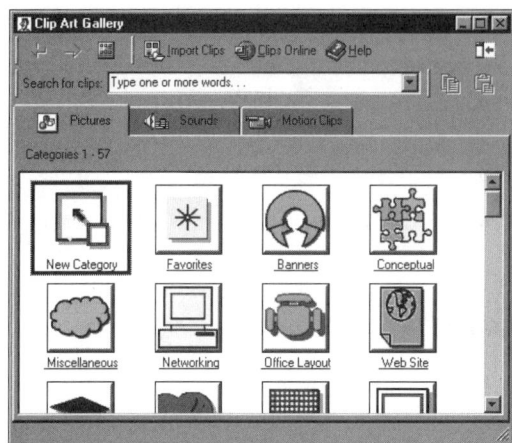

2. Select the tab for the kind of clip art that you want to insert into your Web page.

Be careful with sound and video clips. Unlike graphics, sound and video clips are specific to the various operating systems, such as Windows 95, Macintosh, and UNIX. So if you choose to insert a .wav file in your Web page, for example, Mac and UNIX users will probably not be able to hear it.

3. Choose a category of clip art that interests you. Notice that in the case of sound and video clips, a number of the categories contain no clips.

If you're looking for a specific type of image — say, a birthday graphic — you can enter `birthday` in your search parameters in the Search For Clips field and let FrontPage provide you with a list of clips that meet your search criteria.

4. Click the image that you want to use in your Web page. This brings up a floating menu that gives you four button choices for that piece of clip art:

- **Insert Clip:** Yep, you guessed it. Selecting this button puts the clip in your Web page.

- **Preview Clip:** Select this button to look at or listen to your clip before inserting it into your Web page.

- **Add Clip to Favorite or Other Category:** If you love this clip so much that you keep using it over and over, you can move it to the favorites or another category to make it easier to get to.

- **Find Similar Clips:** Use this option to find other clips that are similar to the one you've currently selected.

To bypass the floating menu altogether, right-click the clip that you want to insert and choose Insert.

Adding Comments to a Web Page

When working in a multi-user environment — or if you're forgetful like me — leaving comments in your Web pages is a good way to stay on top of your work. Comments let you make notes about how you might change text or features in the future or remind you how or why you did something to your HTML file.

Although comments are embedded in the HTML source of a Web page, people using a Web browser to view the Web page can't see them, unless they choose to view the HTML source file itself. To add comments to a Web page, follow these steps:

1. Place the cursor where you want to insert your comment. (You can do so in either the Normal View or the HTML View.)

2. Choose Insert⇨Comment from the menu bar.

3. Insert your comment text in the Comment dialog box, as shown in the following figure.

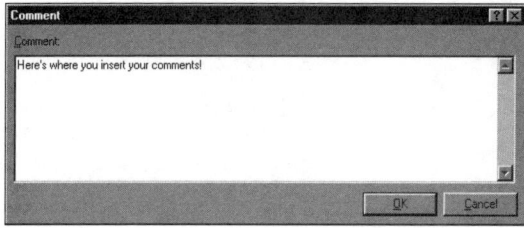

4. Click OK to insert the comment in your Web page.

Comments in the Normal View appear as a text block that you can move anywhere on the page. To move the comments, click and drag the comment block to any location on-screen.

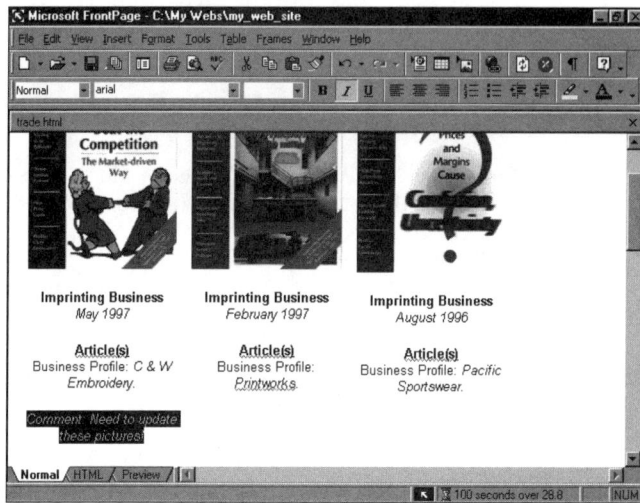

The HTML View displays comments as a snippet of text, surrounded by a series of arrows and Web page commands. This additional text makes the comment text invisible to viewers of the Web page.

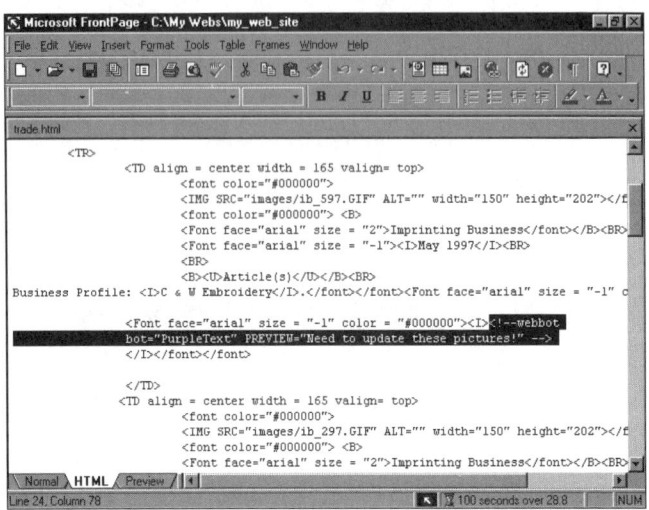

 You can edit the text of a comment in one of two ways. To edit your comment in the Normal View, double-click the text box when the mouse arrow changes to a hand with a piece of paper. In the HTML view, you can exit the comment by editing the text next to the PREVIEW label.

 For a more in-depth discussion of HTML tags, check out *HTML For Dummies,* 3rd Edition, by Ed Tittel and Stephen N. James (IDG Books Worldwide, Inc.).

Adding Components to a Web Page

Because FrontPage 2000 is an official Office product, it comes with a number of features that are similar in both style and name to those of the other Office products. And, like the other Office products, when something differs from the standard set of Office features, it gets a nifty-sounding name that, by itself, doesn't seem to mean much.

The best way to think of the Component features of FrontPage 2000 is as a catchall for cool FrontPage features that don't seem to fit anywhere else. Components are roughly broken down into these four categories:

+ **Office elements:** These are other Office elements, such as Excel spreadsheets and charts that you can generate in a number of other Office programs.

See also Part VI for more information about the Office elements.

✦ **Basic Web elements:** This group of elements includes things like banners, marquees, and hit counters, which track the number of people who visit a Web page.

See also the descriptions of the basic Web elements — Banner Ad Manager, Hit Counter, Hover Button, and Marquee — that are given later in this part.

✦ **Page composition tools:** Use this series of tools to schedule when things like pictures appear in a Web page.

See Part VII for more information about the page composition tools.

✦ **Property management tools:** This series of tools enables you to modify the default properties of objects, such as search forms and categories that are used to track pages in a multi-user environment.

Adding a banner ad

So what is a banner ad, anyway? Well, mostly, it's how companies make their money on the Web — but that's a different story! Actually, a banner is simply a set of similarly sized images, usually appearing either at the top or the bottom of a Web page.

Banners are commonly used as a method of promoting advertising messages, as well as key pieces of information that you want users to know. Adding a banner in FrontPage 2000 is exceptionally simple. Just follow these steps:

1. Choose Insert⇨Component⇨Banner Ad Manager from the menu bar. You see the Banner Ad Manager Properties dialog box, in which you can specify all the different settings for your banner ad.

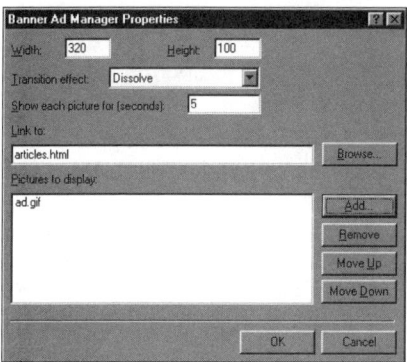

2. Choose the settings for your banner ad. The following table explains the various settings.

Banner Ad Setting	What It Means
Width/Height	The size of the banner. If your images are large, FrontPage crops them to fit.
Transition Effects	How the banner ads transition from one to the next. The more complicated the images are, the slower the page downloads.
Show Each Picture For	The duration of time that users can view each image.
Link To	If you want the banner to link to another page or Web site, specify where you want it to link in this field.
Pictures to Display	Using the Add, Remove, Move Up, and Move Down buttons, you can specify the number of images, as well as their viewing order that you want to display from this area.

3. Click OK to insert the banner ad into your Web page.

4. Select the Preview View in the FrontPage Editor to preview your banner.

Banner ads work by adding a Java applet to your Web. The advantage to using Java is that the ad transitions look nicer. However, if you start using a lot of transitions, adding an applet makes your Web page run slower.

Adding a hit counter

A hit counter tracks the number of times a page has been accessed and displays that number of "hits" on the Web page itself. It's a nice way of saying, "Hey, look how popular my Web page is!" That is, unless nobody's visiting your Web site, in which case you probably don't want to include a hit counter.

To add a hit counter to a Web page, follow these steps:

1. Choose Insert⇨Component⇨Hit Counter from the menu bar. FrontPage displays the Hit Counter Properties dialog box.

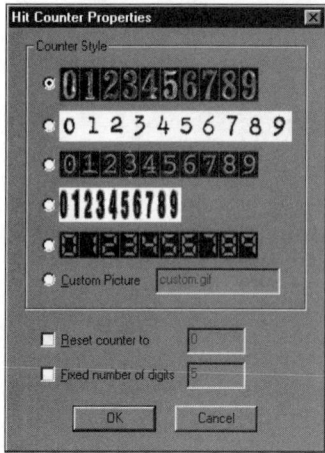

2. Specify the style and number of digits you want in your hit counter.

3. Click OK to insert the hit counter into your Web page.

If you're editing an existing hit counter and you want to reset the counter, check the Reset Counter To check box and, in the field next to it, type the number to which you want to the counter to be reset.

Adding a hover button

If you don't have buttons that animate or highlight when you roll your mouse cursor over them, then something's definitely wrong with your Web site — at least that's what the conventional wisdom preaches. There are a number of methods for adding this kind of graphical quality to a Web page, including using JavaScript and Dynamic HTML. Not to be outdone, FrontPage 2000 offers you a way to use Java to create the same effect!

Here's how you create cool-looking buttons:

1. Choose Insert⇨Component⇨Hover Button from the menu bar. FrontPage 2000 displays the Hover Button Properties dialog box.

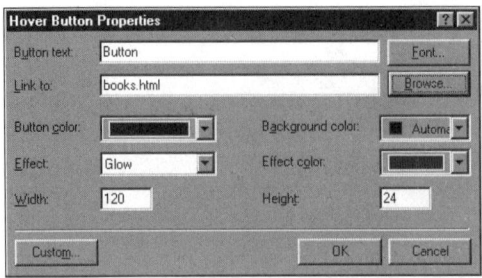

102

2. Specify the properties for your hover button. You can set a number of different options for the button, including the size and color of the button and its highlight state, the *rollover effect* (what happens when the mouse cursor rolls over the button), and the page to which the button links when you click it.

You can also customize your hover button by clicking the Custom button. Here, you can pick rollover and mouse-click sounds and even provide your own rollover graphics.

3. Click OK to insert the hover button into your Web page.

In all honesty, this is not the most efficient way to build animated buttons because it uses Java, which is a memory hog and can slow down even the fastest Web browsers.

For more information about building animated buttons that are lighter and don't use Java, check out *JavaScript For Dummies,* 2nd Edition, by Emily A. Vander Veer (IDG Books Worldwide, Inc.).

Adding a marquee

Have you ever seen the stock listing whoosh by on one of the digital boards or on the bottom of your television screen? Sure you have! Well, those are two examples of marquees, and yes, you can easily embed a marquee in your Web page.

To add a marquee to a Web page in FrontPage 2000, follow these steps:

1. Choose Insert➪Component➪Marquee from the menu bar. FrontPage displays the Marquee Properties dialog box.

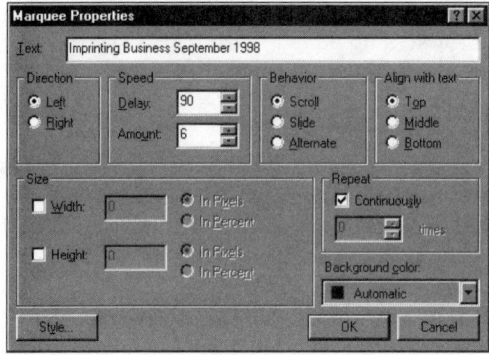

2. Specify the properties for your marquee. The following table explains your options.

Marquee Setting	What It Means
Direction	Specify the direction in which you want the text to move across the screen.
Speed	Choose the speed at which you want the text to move.
Behavior	Indicate how you want the text to move on-screen.
Align with Text	Specify where you want the banner to be located in relation to the text around it.
Size	Choose the size of the banner.
Repeat	Decide whether the banner repeats continuously or just once.
Background Color	Indicate the background color for the banner.

In addition to these options, you can change the text style associated with the banner. To do so, click the Style button and then either choose from the available styles or select Format to create one.

3. Click OK to insert the marquee into your Web page.

Adding Graphics to a Web Page

Now that FrontPage 2000 looks more like Word than anything else, adding graphics to a Web page in FrontPage and adding graphics to a document in Word are nearly identical. That said, you can still use FrontPage's HTML editing capabilities to add graphics, too.

Although FrontPage 2000 supports a host of graphics file formats, many older browsers do not support many of these file types. As a result, you're better off making sure that the graphic you want to import is in either .gif or .jpg format before you import it into FrontPage 2000.

For more information about the basics of the Web, including things like graphic file formats, check out *Creating Web Pages For Dummies,* 4th Edition, by Bud Smith and Arthur Bebak (published by IDG Books Worldwide, Inc.).

Adding graphics through the Normal View

To add a graphic by using FrontPage's graphical user interface, follow these easy steps:

1. Click the location on the active Web page in the Editor where you want to put your graphic. (If your page is blank, your only choice is to place your cursor in the top left-hand corner.)

2. Choose Insert➪Picture➪From File to bring up the Insert Picture dialog box.

You can also add graphics to a Web page via the traditional Windows drag-and-drop interface. To do so, go to the folder on your desktop that houses the graphic that you want to insert. Click and drag the graphic onto the active Web page and voilà! There it is . . . good to go!

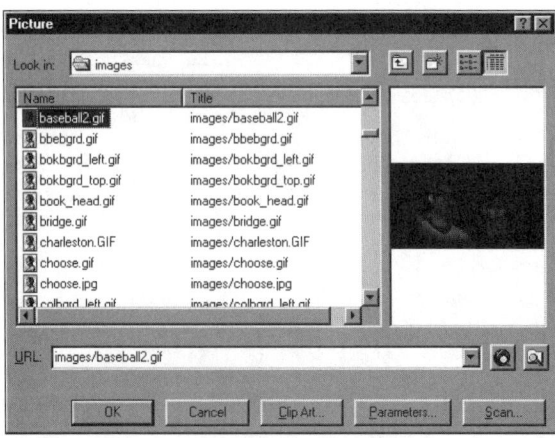

3. Choose the graphic that you want to insert from the Picture dialog box. From the Picture dialog box, you can browse your Web, the rest of your computer, or the Internet to find the graphic that you want to insert. FrontPage 2000 also provides thumbnail previews for each graphic that you click, so you can see what you're adding before you add it. FrontPage 2000 defaults to enabling you to view only the files in your Web. To add graphics from another place, you need to click either the globe with the spyglass (for the Internet) or the folder with a spyglass (for your computer) to choose graphics from files in another location.

You're always better off adding graphics files to your Web before adding them to a Web page. That way, the files are already contained in your Web, and you'll never have to worry about changing the file pathnames of links in the Web pages.

See "Importing Webs and Web Pages" in Part II for more information about adding files to a Web.

4. Click OK to add the graphic to your Web page.

You may have noticed that the Picture dialog box contains a Parameters button. Clicking this button allows you to do two things: One, you can change the link's pathway to the graphic.

In addition, the Parameters dialog box allows you to set string values for each graphic. *String values* are identifiers that get passed along to a database when the user clicks a graphic that is also a link.

For more information about string values and using them in conjunction with Web pages and databases, check out *SQL For Dummies,* 3rd Edition, by Allen G. Taylor (published by IDG Books Worldwide, Inc.).

Adding graphics through the HTML View

Adding graphics through the HTML View is both identical to adding graphics through the Normal View and completely different from that method. By and large, working in the HTML View enables you to use the same menu commands that are available in the Normal View. The basic difference between the two views is appearance. With the Normal View, you see the result graphically. In the HTML View, you see the result in HTML.

You can also add the HTML yourself to generate an item such as a graphic. Adding a graphic in this manner is reasonably straightforward. Just follow these steps:

1. Choose a location in the HTML text to put your graphic.

2. Create an <IMG> tag by typing **<IMG>** in the HTML. This tag contains all the information about your image.

3. Inside the image tag, indicate the location and name of the graphic file by specifying the source of the file. To do so, you need to create a pointer to the file. After the <IMG> tag, type **src="*path location to graphics file*"**. Between the quotes, specify the path location to the graphics file.

For example, to indicate a graphics file in the default images folder, given that the HTML file is in the root directory of your Web, the <IMG> tag syntax would look like this:

```
<IMG src="images/your_image.gif">
```

4. Specify the image and border size for the graphic. Use the `height` and `width` labels to specify the image size. Image size is optional in that, if you don't specify it, the image appears at its regular size. The border label specifies whether the image does or does not have a border, as well as the size of the border. Zero means no border, 1 is a one-point border, and so forth. So, for example, for an image that's 40 pixels by 40 pixels with no border, you'd create the following:

```
<IMG src="images/your_image.gif" width ="40"
     height ="40" border="0">
```

Bookmarking a Page

In FrontPage, bookmarking means something different than it does when you're browsing the World Wide Web. Here, bookmarking means marking an actual spot within a Web page. Why would you do that? You can use the bookmark tool to mark a location on the page for other people on your Web-building team who may be working on the page. For example, if you find an error that some-one else needs to fix, you can bookmark the location of that error. More often than not, however, you'll be creating hyperlinks that will send users to a bookmarked location on a page when they click that link.

Here's how to add a bookmark to a Web page:

1. In the Normal View, place the cursor where you want the bookmark to go.

2. Choose Insert⇨Bookmark from the menu bar. The Bookmark dialog box appears.

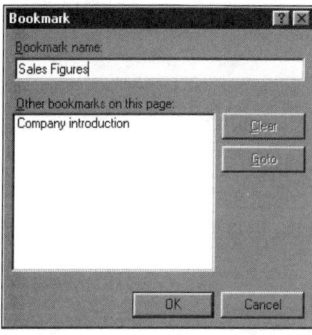

3. Type a name for the bookmark in the Bookmark Name box.

4. Click OK to add the bookmark to the Web page. After you add the bookmark, an icon appears in the Normal View, indicating the location of the bookmark that you added. In the HTML View, the following text is added to the Web page when you add a bookmark:

```
<a name = "name_of_bookmark"></a>
```

See "Hyperlinks" later in this part to find out how to link a book-mark on a page.

> **TIP** If you have multiple bookmarks on a page that's quite long, you can jump to a bookmark by bringing up the Bookmark dialog box, selecting the bookmark that you want to visit, and clicking the Goto button.

Converting Text to a Table and Back Again

One of the fundamental components of Web design is the table. Before the advent of programs like FrontPage 2000, most Web design was done by constructing large and elaborate tables — and tables within tables — to achieve a desired effect.

Although tables can be made to look compelling, the work is, well, tedious. Thankfully for all of us, with FrontPage, you can eliminate a lot of the tedium simply by using FrontPage's Convert function. With the Convert tool, you can convert any bit of text into a table and go back again, taking tables and reverting them to strictly text.

See "Tables" later in this part for more information about more of FrontPage's table features.

To convert text to a table, follow these steps:

1. Highlight the text that you want to convert to a table.

2. Choose Table⇨Convert⇨Text to Table. FrontPage brings up the Convert Text To Table dialog box.

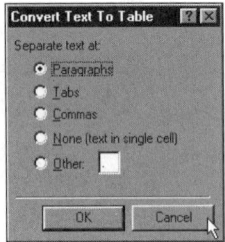

3. Choose a method of conversion for the highlighted text. You can create a table from text in a number of ways:

• **Paragraphs:** FrontPage creates new rows in the table based on paragraph returns.

• **Tabs:** FrontPage creates a new cell in a row for every tab and then generates a new row at every paragraph return.

• **Commas:** Works just like the Tabs method, except this method uses commas to separate the cell data.

• **None:** This method puts all the highlighted text into one cell in one row of data.

- **Other:** This method uses a character marker in your text to create new rows. For example, you can specify that every time FrontPage comes across a new period (.), it creates a new cell.

4. Click OK to convert your text to a table.

Once you've created a table, converting it back to text is even simpler. In the Normal View, highlight the table and choose Table➪Convert➪Table to Text.

HTML Properties

Although most of the attention in FrontPage 2000 is paid to the Normal View, the HTML View is where the raw HTML coding takes place. Changes made to the Web page are ultimately made in the HTML View. In fact, you don't need to use the Normal View at all. If you want, you can go right to the HTML View and code HTML just as if you were using any other HTML editor.

To that end, a number of options pertain directly to HTML that you can set in FrontPage. You set these options in the Page Options dialog box, which you access by choosing Tools➪Page Options from the menu bar.

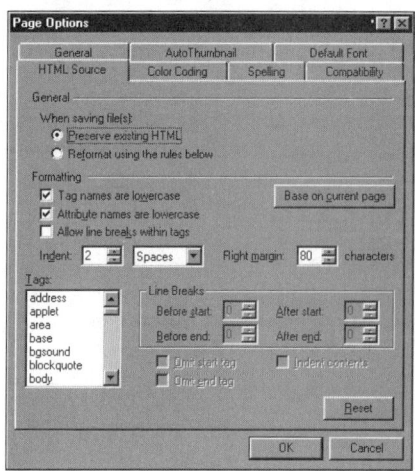

Setting HTML source options

Because FrontPage 2000 is new to the Office suite, a great many people will be coming to the software already having functioning Web sites built in other programs. Although you may be ready to use a graphical interface for building Web pages, you may not be ready for FrontPage to go in and start changing the HTML that you've already created.

Fortunately, you can tell FrontPage exactly how to handle the HTML source in Web pages that you've already created. Follow these steps:

1. Choose Tools➪Page Options. The Page Options dialog box appears.

2. Select the HTML Source tab.

3. In the General area, select an option for HTML preservation when saving files. You have two options: keep the HTML the way it is, or reformat the HTML according to a series of rules that you specify. FrontPage defaults to keeping your HTML just the way it is, right down to the capitalization on the tags. However, if you want to reformat the HTML, you have the following options in the Formatting area of the HTML Source tab:

• Set the tags (<a> . . . </a>, for example) to all lower-case by checking the Tag Names Are Lowercase box.

• Set all the attributes (for example, href=" ") to lowercase by checking the Attribute Names Are Lowercase box.

• Choose to allow line breaks within individual tags by checking the Allow Line Breaks within Tags box.

• Specify how far to indent the HTML source and set a right margin in the Indent and Right Margin drop-down lists.

• For the 56 different tags that FrontPage includes in the options page (depending on the tag type), you can specify the locations of the line breaks, specify whether to use the indent controls, and set the start and end tag options.

• You can also click the Base on Current Page button to set the HTML options to mirror the page you're currently working on.

My advice on this one is: *Don't!* Although having this amount of flexibility is nice, leaving the HTML alone is always the best choice. That way, you ensure that nothing gets changed inadvertently.

4. Click OK to enable the new HTML source changes.

Setting HTML color coding options

HTML would be really hard to read if it were all black. To combat this, FrontPage allows you to color-code various elements of the HTML code so that you can tell them apart.

To set the color options for the HTML, follow these steps:

1. Choose Tools➪Page Options. The Page Options dialog box appears.

2. Select the Color Coding tab.

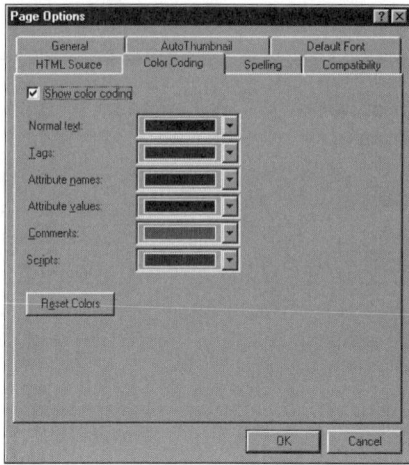

3. Specify the color that you want for each option shown. You can specify a color for each of the following HTML source elements:

- **Normal Text:** The bulk of the text in the HTML source. This option does not set the color for what users see, only for what you see in the FrontPage Editor.

- **Tags:** This option sets the color for all the tags in the HTML source, such as <HTML>. . . </HTML>.

- **Attribute Names:** Attributes are embedded within the HTML tags and include things like HREF and SRC.

For more information about <HTML> tags and other elements of HTML coding, check out *HTML For Dummies.*

- **Attribute Values:** Each attribute is connected to an equal sign and quotes with a specific value between the quotes. This option sets the color for those values.

- **Comments:** Comments are the notes to yourself, or the notes that FrontPage inserts, that users never see.

- **Scripts:** This option sets the color for things like JavaScript code, Java code, and VB Script code.

In addition to these choices, you can turn off color coding altogether by deselecting the Show Color Coding check box.

4. Click OK from the Page Options dialog box to make the new color coding changes.

Hyperlinks

Hyperlinks sounds like such an impressive word . . . very futuristic . . . the kind of thing you'd expect Captain Kirk or Captain Picard to burst out with on any given episode of *Star Trek*. Truthfully, though, hyperlinks are just a way of jumping from location to location within a series of Web pages.

Hyperlinks are the navigational building blocks of any Web site. Without hyperlinks, you'd never get off the home page of a Web site. So it should come as no surprise that FrontPage has a vast array of tools for generating and maintaining hyperlinks.

See "Recalculating a Project's Hyperlinks" in Part III for more information about how FrontPage can help you manage the hyperlinks in your Web site.

To create a hyperlink in a Web page, follow these steps:

1. Highlight the text or image that you want to turn into a hyperlink. You can also create a link to a page without highlighting anything at all. In this case, the link uses the title of the page that you're linking to for a text description.

2. Choose Insert➪Hyperlink from the menu bar to bring up the Create Hyperlink dialog box.

If you're trying to cut down on using menus, you can press Ctrl+K to bring up the Create Hyperlink dialog box instead. You can also click the button shown to the left on the Standard Toolbar to access the dialog box.

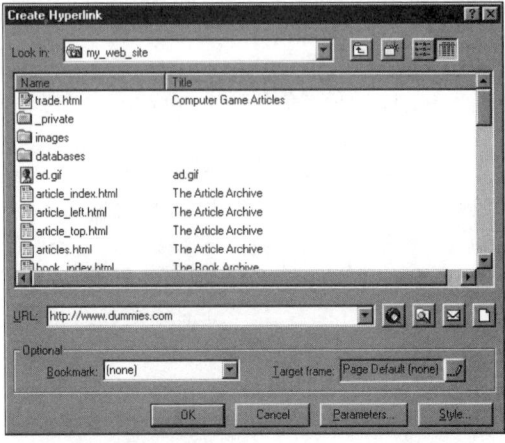

3. Enter the link location in the URL field. FrontPage has five options for linking to pages and objects:

- **Browsing your Web:** FrontPage enables you to browse through your Web by using a pull-down menu and to select a page or an object to link to.

- **Using a Web browser:** If you click the globe button in the Create Hyperlink dialog box, FrontPage launches your default Web browser. With your browser open, you can search for the Web page that you want to link to and then insert it in the URL field.

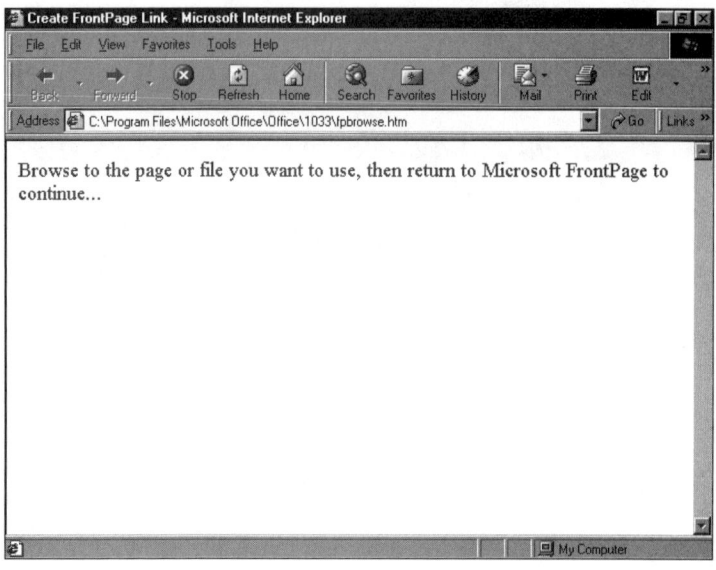

- **Browsing your computer:** Clicking the file folder with a spyglass lets you browse your entire computer for files, as opposed to looking for files only within the current Web. When you double-click a file that you want to link to, the pathway to the file is placed in the URL field.

Although browsing your computer may be a good way to create links to files on an intranet, where everyone has access to the same files on a network server, it's a very bad way to link to files when publishing to a Web site. FrontPage inserts an absolute pathway to a file that includes the drive letter (C:, D:, and so on). If the files are on your local machine, the link won't work when it's posted to your Web site. The only instance in which this is not the case is when your PC *is* the Web server.

- **Inserting an e-mail address:** If you click the e-mail button in the Create Hyperlink dialog box, you can enter an e-mail address to serve as the link. In this case, when a user clicks the link, the browser launches the default e-mail client and inserts the specified address in the To: field of a message.

- **Creating a new page and linking to it:** FrontPage 2000 also enables you to create a new page and generate a link to that page. You can accomplish this by clicking the New Page icon to the far right of the Edit Hyperlink dialog box. Doing so brings up the New dialog box, which enables you to create the new page. (*See also* "Creating Web Pages" in Part II.)

4. Click OK to insert the link into your Web page.

Linking to a bookmark on a Web page

Sometimes, you may want to send a person not to just another page in your Web, but rather to a specific point on a Web page. With FrontPage 2000's bookmark and hyperlink features, sending someone to a specific point on a Web page is a snap!

Here's how you do it:

1. Choose Insert⇨Hyperlink to bring up the Create Hyperlink dialog box. You can also press Ctrl+K or click the hyperlink button on the Standard Toolbar.

2. Browse your Web for the page that you want to link to and then click it once to select it. If the page has a bookmark on it, the name of the bookmark shows up in the Optional area in the Bookmark drop-down list.

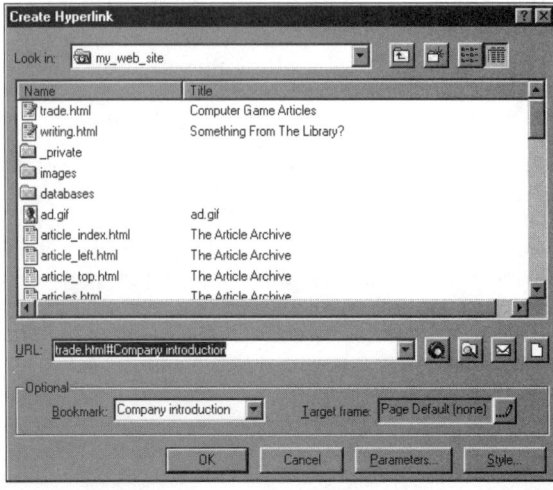

3. Choose your bookmark. Once you've chosen a bookmark, FrontPage inserts the proper reference to the bookmark at the end of the link page in the URL field.

4. Click OK to insert the link with a bookmark.

See "Bookmarking a Page" earlier in this part for more information about adding a bookmark to a page.

Creating a link in the HTML View

Although using the Normal View is nice, every now and then you may need to create a link the old-fashioned way, in HTML. To create a link in the HTML View, follow these steps:

1. Find the location in your HTML that you want to place a link.

2. Create an ⟨A⟩ tag.

For more information about <A> tags and other elements of HTML coding, check out *HTML For Dummies,* by Ed Tittel and Stephen N. James.

3. Within the ⟨A⟩ tag, create an HREF label to serve as the pointer for the location that you're going to link to. The HREF label must be followed by an = sign, and the link location must be surrounded by quotation marks, in the following manner:

```
<A HREF="http://www.dummies.com">
```

4. Following the ⟨A⟩ tag, insert the text to describe the link. For example, a link to the *...For Dummies* Web site would look something like this:

```
<A HREF="http://www.dummies.com"> The Home of
    the ...For Dummies Books
```

5. Close the link by including an ⟨/A⟩ tag. When it's all said and done, you should have something that looks like this:

```
<A HREF="http://www.dummies.com"> The Home of
    the ...For Dummies Books </A>
```

Check out *Creating Web Pages For Dummies Quick Reference* by Doug Lowe (published by IDG Books Worldwide, Inc.) for more tips on creating elements in HTML.

Navigation Bars

If you're really in a hurry and you don't even remotely care what your Web site looks like, adding a Navigation Bar through FrontPage may be the perfect solution for you. FrontPage Navigation Bars aren't pretty (not by a longshot), but they are functional, and they offer a quick way to set up site navigation.

Adding Navigation Bars automatically through FrontPage really only works if you're using the Navigation View to organize your Web site into logical content groupings.

See "Organizing Project Pages" in Part III for more information about using the Navigation View.

To add a Navigation Bar, follow these steps:

1. Make sure that your Web page is included in its proper location within the Web hierarchy. You can do so in the Navigation View.

2. Choose Insert➪Navigation Bar from the menu bar. FrontPage displays the Navigation Bar Properties dialog box.

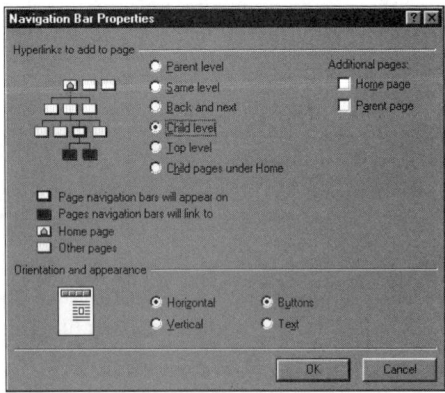

3. Choose the appropriate hyperlink level setup for the Navigation Bar. The following table explains your options.

Hyperlink Option	What It Means
Parent Level	The level above the current page
Same Level	Any other pages at the same level as the page you're currently working in
Back and Next	The pages directly to your left and right on the same level

Hyperlink Option	What It Means
Child Level	Any pages for which the page in which you're inserting the Navigation Bar is the parent
Top Level	Pages at the very top level of the site, including the home page and any others at that level
Child Pages under Home	Pages on the level below the top (home page) level

> *Note:* You can also choose to add links to both the Home page and the Parent page by selecting the appropriate check box in the Navigation Bar Properties dialog box.

4. Select a button style in the Orientation and Appearance area of the Navigation Properties dialog box. You can use either text buttons or standard Web buttons and change the orientation of the buttons to be either horizontal or vertical.

5. Click OK to insert the new Navigation Bar.

Page Banners

Page banners are a quick and easy way to add titles to your Web pages. To add a page banner, follow these steps:

1. Place your cursor in the location on the page where you want to insert the banner.

2. Choose Insert⇨Page Banner from the menu bar. The Page Banner Properties dialog box appears.

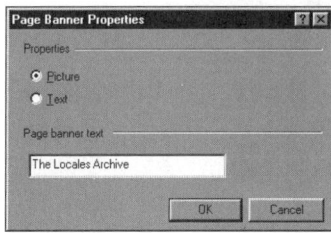

3. Select whether you want the banner to be treated as plain text (select the Text radio button) or as an image (select the Picture radio button).

4. Insert a title for your banner in the Page Banner Text field.

5. Click OK to insert the banner.

If you're using shared borders, you can set up a banner in a shared area, and FrontPage will apply it across all the pages sharing that border. This is a quick and easy way to create a title and put it on many pages at the same time.

Page Compatibility

One of the biggest complaints people have had with previous versions of FrontPage deals with compatibility. Time and again, users have complained that FrontPage generated HTML and scripts that weren't particularly compatible with non-Microsoft browsers and servers.

To combat those sentiments, FrontPage 2000 allows users to set the browser, server, and technology compatibility of an individual page. When that compatibility is set, FrontPage enables only those HTML commands and features that conform to the compatibility options.

To set your page compatibility settings, follow these steps:

1. Choose Tools⇨Page Options to bring up the Page Options dialog box.

2. Select the Compatibility tab.

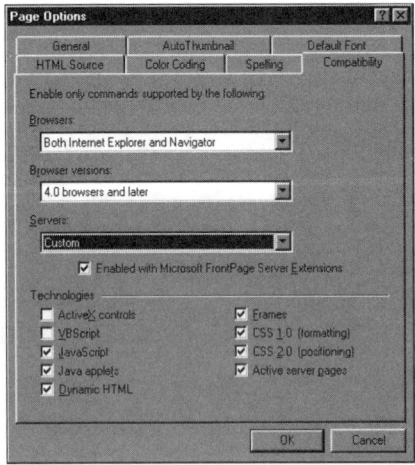

3. Choose your browser and server settings. The browser question comes down to a few key choices:

- **Browsers:** Which browsers do you want to support? From the drop-down list, you can choose to support only Internet Explorer, only Netscape Navigator, both browsers, or only the Microsoft WebTV.

- **Browser Versions:** FrontPage breaks up browser versions into a simple 3.0 and 4.0 distinction. If you want to support the 3.0 browsers, a great number of the newer features like Dynamic HTML and Cascading Style Sheets won't be available to you.

- **Servers:** You probably don't need to worry too much about this option, but it allows you to choose between supporting Microsoft Web servers and Apache servers. The smart answer is to choose both, which you get by choosing Custom.

4. Choose your technology settings in the Technologies area. FrontPage lets you control nine different technology areas via a check box.

   See Part VII for more information about these nine technology areas.

5. Click OK to enable the new page compatibility settings.

Page Properties

Every Web page has a number of individual options that you can modify to fit the needs of the site you're building. These options range from choosing Web page background images to specifying the color of hyperlinks. FrontPage organizes these options in one convenient place so that accessing them is a snap.

In the Normal View, you can right-click in a Web page and choose Page Properties to access this tabbed dialog box, called Page Properties.

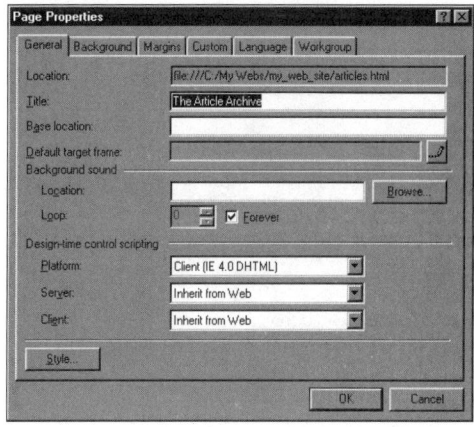

You can do a number of detailed things from the Page Properties dialog box, most of which are described in the following sections. Some of the simpler options that you can easily change include the following:

✦ **Changing a page title:** You can change a page title by inputting a new name in the <u>T</u>itle field on the General tab.

✦ **Specifying a default page sound:** Also on the General tab, you can click the <u>B</u>rowse button to place a sound in your Web. Unless you leave the <u>F</u>orever box unchecked and insert a value in the Loop field, the sound will loop continuously when the page is loaded.

Sounds are platform-dependent, so if you specify a PC sound file (for example, a .wav file), Macintosh and UNIX Web users won't hear it.

✦ **Specifying the page language:** On the Language tab, you can choose the language for both the page text and the HTML coding.

✦ **Assigning categories to the page:** Categories are used to track a page when it's being worked on in a multi-user environment. On the Workgroup tab, you can specify the categories that a page falls under, as well as the current review status of the page and who's assigned to work on it.

See Part III for more information about categories and how to use them.

Setting a background image

To set a background image from the Page Properties dialog box (which you access by right-clicking in a Web page in the Normal View and choosing Page Properties), follow these steps:

1. Select the Background tab.

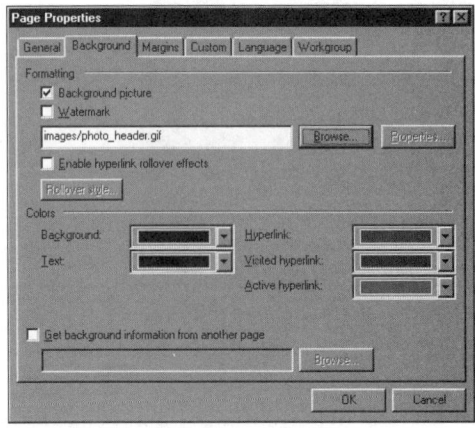

2. In the Formatting area, select the Background P<u>i</u>cture check box.

3. Click the <u>B</u>rowse button to locate and select the background image that you want to use.

When you click this button, the Select Background Picture dialog box appears, as shown in the following figure. Like every other dialog box in FrontPage that requires you to find a file, the Select Background Picture dialog box defaults to letting you choose files from your Web only. However, by clicking either the globe button or the file folder button, you can look for background images on the Web or elsewhere on your computer as well. You can also click the Clip Art button to bring up the Clip Art Gallery to find an image from there.

See also "Adding Clip Art to a Web Page," earlier in this part.

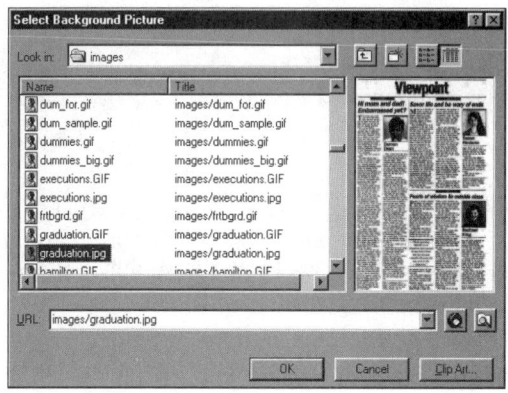

4. Click OK. The image you chose won't be visible until you click OK to close the Page Properties dialog box, too.

 If you've already set a background image for another page on your Web site, you can use the same background image for the page you're currently in by importing the page settings. To do so, check the Get Background Information from Another Page box and then click the Browse button to find the page from which you want to import the page settings.

 If you choose to import a background image, your background colors and hyperlink colors (see the following section) will also be imported.

 If you're using a theme, you'll find that the Background tab in the Page pProperties dialog box is missing. That's because you're using a theme, and themes require that all the pages using the theme have the same background settings.

Setting background colors

From the Background tab in the Page Properties dialog box, you can set the background colors and the various hyperlink colors for a Web page. For each option, a drop-down list enables you to choose from a series of default colors, as well as to specify your own Web-safe color through the color picker, shown in the following figure.

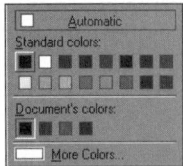

In total, there are five color options:

+ **Background:** If you don't have a background image selected, this color appears on the page.

+ **Text:** This menu sets the default color for text on your Web page.

+ **Hyperlink:** The hyperlink color is the color that is shown for either text that represents a link or the border around an image that's a link. This color is shown only if the link has never been visited.

+ **Visited Hyperlink:** Identical to the Hyperlink, except this color is displayed if a link *has* been previously visited.

+ **Active Hyperlink:** This color appears on a link when a user clicks it.

Setting page margins

Say you want to indent an entire Web page, either from the top or from the left. What might otherwise be a bear of an HTML problem, FrontPage 2000 makes an exceptionally trivial task. Here's how you do it:

1. From the Page Properties dialog box (which you access by right-clicking a Web page in the Normal View and then choosing Page Properties), select the Margins tab.

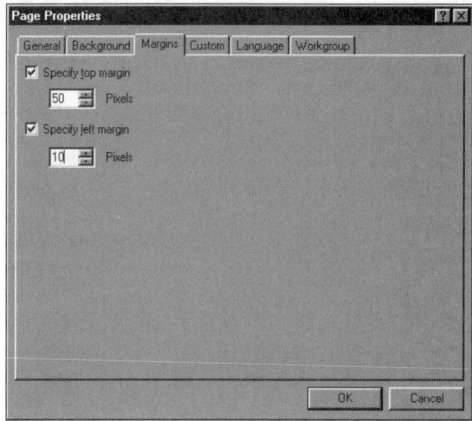

2. Check the box of the margin that you want to indent. FrontPage lets you indent only the top and left-hand margins.

3. In the Pixels fields, type the desired margin size.

4. Click OK to see how your new margins look!

See "Changing Text Attributes" earlier in this part for more information about setting spacing for text and paragraphs.

Page Transitions and Animations

One of the more interesting features of FrontPage 2000 is the capability to add transitions into and out of Web pages. Transitions, which are common in presentation software like PowerPoint, include such things as wipes, fades, and reveals. They add drama to an otherwise boring Web link interaction.

Follow these steps to add a transition on a Web page:

1. Choose Format⇨Page Transition from the menu bar to bring up the Page Transitions dialog box.

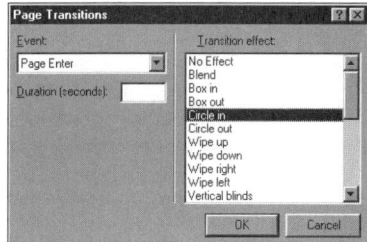

2. Select a transition event and the transition effect. Four events can trigger a page transition element: page entrance/exit and site entrance/exit. For each event, you have 25 different transitions to choose from.

3. Set the length of the transition in the Duration (Seconds) field.

4. Click OK to insert the transition.

 These transitions may look nice and work well with current versions of Internet Explorer (4.0 or above), but they don't work with Netscape Navigator.

Spell-Checking as You Work

FrontPage 2000 is a mirror image of Microsoft Word where spelling is concerned. Just like in Word, you press F7 to spell-check a page. Similarly, you press Shift+F7 to pull up the Thesaurus.

In addition to these tasks, you can set a few other spelling options in the Page Options dialog box. To do so, follow these steps:

1. Choose Tools⇨Page Options from the menu bar. The Page Options dialog box appears.

2. Select the Spelling tab.

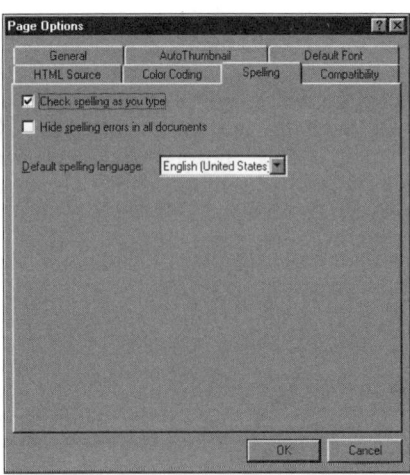

3. Set your spelling options. You can tell FrontPage to check your spelling as you type, as well as to hide the spelling errors in your page. In addition, you can specify the dictionary that you want to use for spell-checking.

4. Click OK to enable the new spelling settings.

Tables

Tables are the backbone of nearly all Web page development. The notion of a table with rows and columns was one of the first concepts introduced in the very first version of HTML. Even with the advent of Dynamic HTML, Cascading Style Sheets, and a host of plug-ins, tables are still the simplest way of presenting data within a Web browser.

Not surprisingly, FrontPage offers a host of utilities that make generating and maintaining tables a reasonably easy task. It should also come as no surprise that the syntax and methodology for creating tables is very similar to that in the other Office programs.

Creating a new table

To create a table in FrontPage, follow these steps:

1. Choose Table⇨Insert⇨Table from the menu bar. The Insert Table dialog box appears.

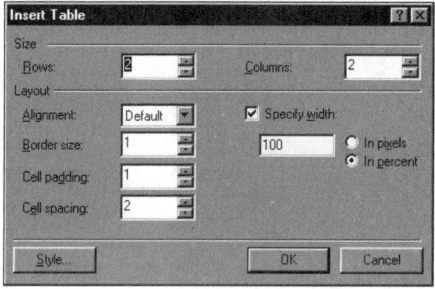

2. Choose the number of Rows and Columns that you want for your table.

   Remember: If you need more rows and columns after you create your table, you can just right-click a cell and choose Insert Row or Insert Column from the pop-up menu.

3. Set your layout options. You have the following five options in the layout area of the Insert Table dialog box:

   • **Alignment:** Sets how you want the table to be aligned on the page. Choices are left, right, center, and justify.

   • **Border Size:** Sets a line border around both the cells and the outside of the table. If you don't want a border, set the value to 0.

- **Cell Padding:** Sets the distance, in pixels, between the borders of a cell and the text within the cell.

- **Cell Spacing:** Sets the distance, in pixels, between cells.

- **Specify Width:** Sets the width of the table. You can specify the width as a percentage of the page or as a set pixel width.

You can also set the text style for the table by clicking the Style button. *See also* "Building Pages by Using Style Sheets" in Part VII.

4. Click OK to insert the new table.

Once you've created a table, you can go back and change the properties you just set by placing your cursor in any table cell and then choosing Table⇨Properties⇨Table to bring up the Table Properties dialog box.

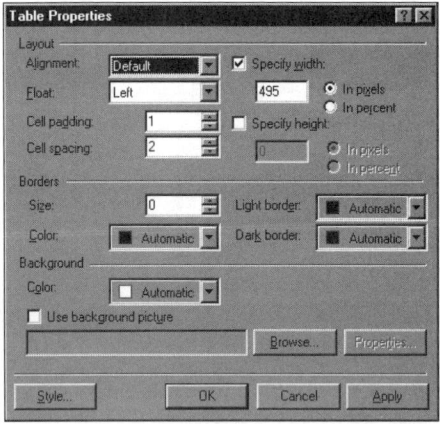

You can also choose Table⇨Properties⇨Cell to change the properties you just set for individual cells. Make your changes in the Cell Properties dialog box that appears.

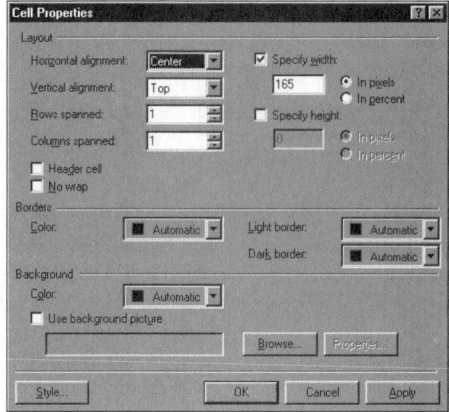

Creating a table by using Draw Table

FrontPage 2000 has a cool little feature called Draw Table that enables you to hand-draw a table by using a pencil tool and a floating toolbar. Choose Table⇨Draw Table from the menu bar to access this feature.

The following figure describes what each of the toolbar buttons enables you to do.

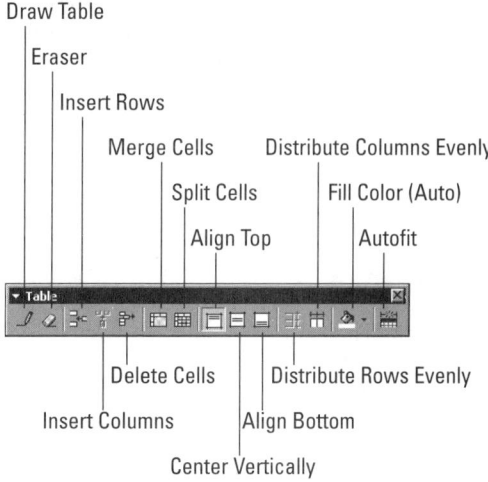

Modifying tables

In addition to generating tables, FrontPage offers a host of tools for modifying tables after you create them. The following is a list of the ways in which you can modify a table:

✦ **Adding cells:** You can add individual cells, rows, or columns. In all cases, first place the cursor where you want to create the new cells, rows, or columns.

- To insert new cells, choose Table⇨Insert⇨Cell. FrontPage places a new cell directly to the right of the cell in which you placed the cursor.

- To insert new rows or columns, choose Table⇨Insert⇨Rows or Columns. The Insert Rows or Columns dialog box appears. Choose the number of rows or columns that you want to insert, as well as their location, and then click OK to insert them.

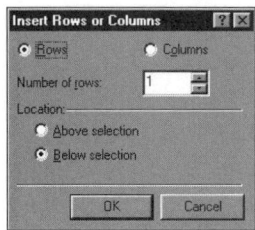

✦ **Deleting cells:** Select a cell (or group of cells) and then choose Table⇨Delete Cells to eliminate the cell and its contents from the table.

✦ **Merging cells:** Select the cells that you want to merge and then choose Table⇨Merge Cells to collapse the two cells and combine their contents.

✦ **Splitting cells:** Select the cells that you want to split and then choose Table⇨Split Cells. From the Split Cells dialog box, choose whether you want to split into rows or columns and how many rows or columns you want to split the cell(s) into, and then click OK.

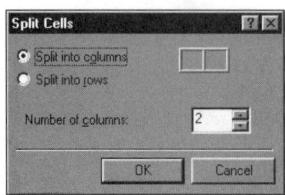

✦ **Distributing cells:** Select rows or columns of uneven size and then choose either Table⇨Distribute Rows Evenly or Table⇨Distribute Columns Evenly to make the rows or columns equal sizes.

✦ **AutoFit:** AutoFit tries to find the optimal size for the cells in the table based on their contents. This way, there's no wasted space in the table. Oftentimes, this is a good tool to use when you've replaced text or a graphic of a different size within a table cell. Select the cells and choose Table➪AutoFit to set the optimal table.

Text Attributes

FrontPage 2000, by and large, looks and feels like Microsoft Word when it comes to changing text attributes. In the Normal View, creating text is as simple as placing the cursor where you want it on-screen and then typing away. Editing your newly typed text is merely a matter of selecting the text and then choosing the appropriate text-editing feature.

But the flexibility that FrontPage offers in changing text attributes does come with a price. In making FrontPage 2000's text-editing features comparable to Word's, Microsoft has committed itself to the latest browser technology. As a result, a number of the advanced text-editing options beyond boldface, italics, and alignment have absolutely no visual effect on older Web browsers, including even Internet Explorer 3.0 and Netscape Navigator 3.0.

The tradeoff boils down to weighing ease-of-use and graphical quality against supporting a larger number of browsers and, therefore, users. In the following sections, I've noted with Warning icons where you're likely to have the biggest pitfalls with the older browsers.

Most of the FrontPage 2000 text attributes are based on the HTML 3.2 and Cascading Style Sheets 2.0 specifications. These two specifications were designed to give Web developers such as yourself greater flexibility in controlling the look of text on-screen. Unfortunately, these two standards are fully supported only through Netscape Communicator 4.0 (and higher) and Internet Explorer 4.0 (and higher).

See Part VII for more information about Cascading Style Sheets.

You can change most of the basic attributes of a piece of text by highlighting it and then selecting the appropriate button from the Formatting Toolbar, as shown in the following figure.

| Normal ▼ | (default font) ▼ | Normal ▼ | **B** *I* <u>U</u> | ☰ ☰ ☰ ☰ | ⅓≣ ☰ 毛 毛 | 🖉 ▾ **A** ▾ |

Changing font properties

To change the text attributes for text that you've created in the Normal View, follow these steps:

1. Highlight the text that you want to change.

2. Choose Format⇨Font from the menu bar. The Font dialog box appears.

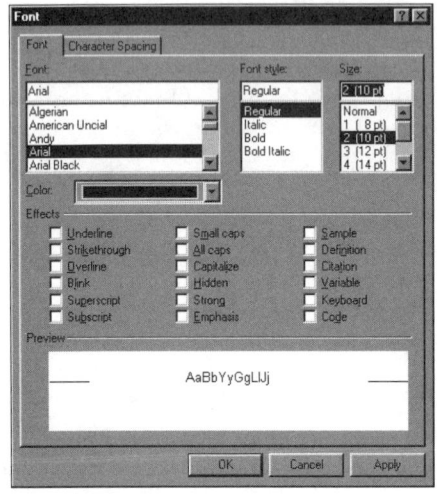

3. Choose the new attributes for the selected text. On the Font and Character spacing tabs, you can change the font type, style, color, and size, as well as modify things like character positioning and spacing. You can also choose from a number of effects, which allow you to modify things like the text's visibility and its emphasis.

One of the biggest problems with Web site development involves fonts. When you change fonts through the Font dialog box, you're changing to fonts that are installed on *your* machine! Those fonts may not be installed on someone else's machine. As a result, what the user sees may be entirely different from what you saw when you created the page. The two safest fonts to use are Arial and Times New Roman.

Many of the items in the Effects category do not work with the older 3.0 browsers.

4. Click OK to enable your text changes.

Changing paragraph settings

To change the paragraph setting for a chunk of text, follow these steps:

1. Highlight the text that you want to change.

2. Choose Format⇨Paragraph from the menu bar. The Paragraph dialog box appears.

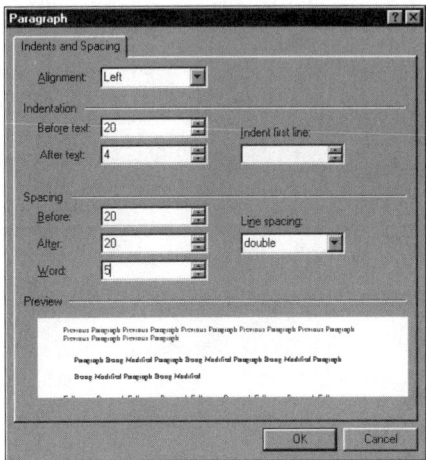

3. Enter the new paragraph settings in the Paragraph dialog box. You can change the alignment, line spacing, and indentation.

Like font attributes, paragraph settings use Cascading Style Sheets and newer versions of HTML to set property values, making many of these settings non-functional with the 3.0 and lower versions of Netscape Navigator and Internet Explorer.

4. Click OK to change the paragraph settings.

Creating bulleted and numbered lists

Bulleted and numbered lists are a simple yet effective way to communicate an idea or concept with emphasis. To turn a series of text items into a bulleted or numbered list, follow these steps:

1. Highlight the text that you want to change.

2. Choose Format⇨Bullets and Numbering from the menu bar to bring up the Bullets and Numbering dialog box.

3. Select the appropriate tab for the kind of list that you want. FrontPage provides three basic kinds of lists: picture bulleted, plain bulleted, and numbered.

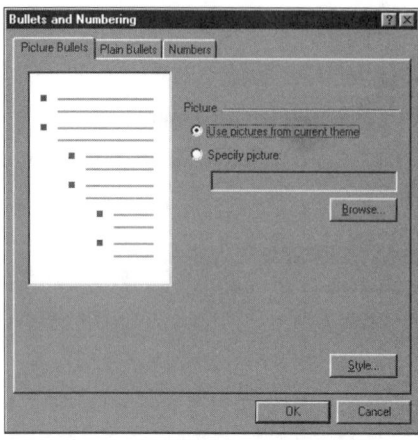

4. Select the bullet or number style that you want.

5. Click OK to change the text to a bulleted or numbered list.

In addition to using the traditional drop-down menus and dialog boxes for formatting bulleted and numbered lists, you can find icons for them on the Formatting Toolbar, directly to the right of the text alignment buttons.

This feature may not work on some of the older browsers, like Netscape Navigator 3.0 and Internet Explorer 3.0.

Changing borders and shading properties

FrontPage 2000 gives you a number of varying text border and shading options. The value in changing these settings is that you can create more emphasis on a particular piece of text by contrasting it with other text elements. Putting emphasis on particular pieces of text is especially useful for important elements that you want visitors to your site to see, such as navigation menus, sidebars, and forms.

To change the border and shading properties, follow these steps:

1. Highlight the text that you want to change.

2. Choose Format⇨Borders and Shading from the menu bar. The Borders and Shading dialog box appears.

3. From the Borders tab, specify the border style that you want for the text box. You have a number of options to choose from:

• **Setting:** Choose from one of three options: no border, a complete border around the text, or a custom border.

• **Style:** Choose a border style — solid lines, dashed lines, and groove lines (my favorite) just to name a few.

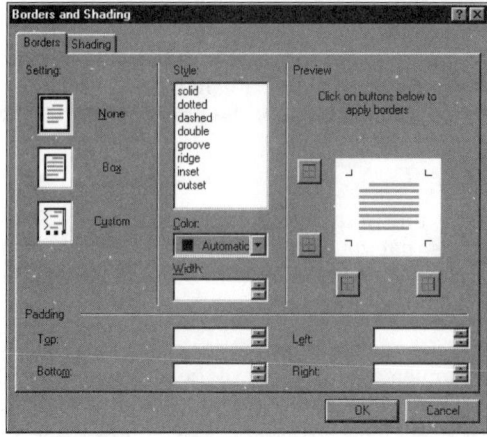

- **Color:** Choose a Web-safe color for your border.

- **Width:** Specify how wide (in pixels) you want the border to be.

- **Padding:** Set how much padding (in pixels) you want between all sides of the border and the text inside it.

- **Preview:** See what your borders will look like, as well as add or remove individual sides of the border.

4. Choose your shading options. From the Shading tab, you can set the foreground and background colors, as well as select an image as the background for the text box. To choose a background image, click the Browse button to find an image on your local drive, a network drive, or the World Wide Web. With each color selection, you have several default choices, but you can also specify any color from the Web palette.

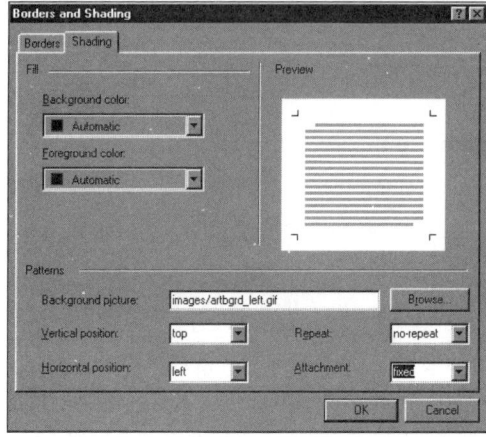

5. Click OK to set your border and shading options.

 All the HTML code required to create these effects are from HTML 3.2 and Cascading Style Sheets 1.0 or higher. As a result, the older 3.0 browsers do not support most of the border and shading options.

Wrapping text

Wrapping text is one of the more unique features of FrontPage 2000. The idea is that you can specify exactly how text should react when it comes into contact with other elements on the page — say, graphics.

Wrapping text is a concept born out of desktop publishing programs and has been implemented as part of the Cascading Style Sheet specification. (*See* Part VII for more information about Cascading Style Sheets.) To set a text-wrapping style, follow these steps:

1. Highlight the text that you want to wrap.

2. Choose Format➪Position to bring up the Position dialog box.

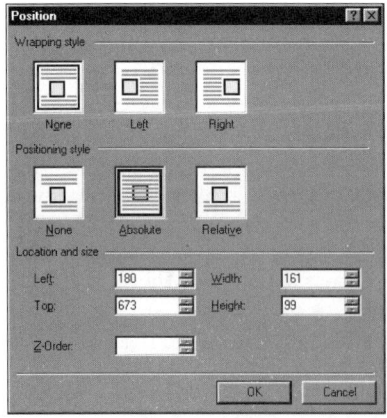

3. Select the wrapping style for the text selection.

4. Set the positioning location.

5. Click OK to set the wrapping style for the text.

 The problem with text wrapping is that it's not particularly well developed in the Cascading Style Sheets spec and not very well implemented in FrontPage 2000. As a result, you often get completely unintended results from attempting to wrap text. It takes a lot of fidgeting to get right.

Part V

Image Editing in FrontPage 2000

Sometimes, just adding an image to a Web page isn't enough. That's why FrontPage 2000 comes with a suite of image-editing and manipulation tools. In this part, you can find out exactly what features the image-editing tools include and how you can use them to edit your own Web graphics.

In this part . . .

- ✓ Using Auto Thumbnails
- ✓ Changing the brightness and contrast of images
- ✓ Adding image maps
- ✓ Rotating and flipping images
- ✓ Scaling images
- ✓ Scanning images
- ✓ Specifying a graphics editor

Activating the Picture Toolbar

In FrontPage 2000, you can't edit a graphics image without first activating the Picture Toolbar. Unlike a number of the other toolbars in FrontPage, the Picture Toolbar does not have corresponding keyboard or menu options. To activate the Picture Toolbar, choose View➪Toolbars➪Picture.

The following figure shows the basic function of each button on the Picture Toolbar.

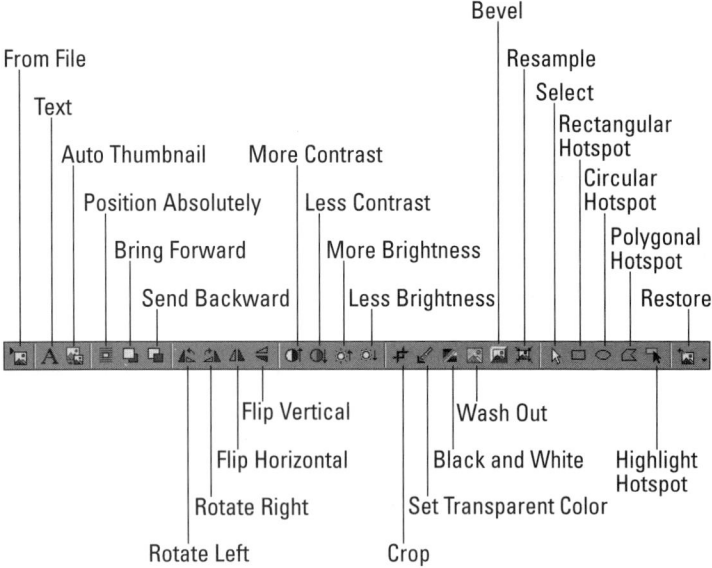

You can customize the Picture Toolbar to have only the features you want on it. To do so, click the down-arrow button to the right of the toolbar. The Add or Remove Buttons menu appears. Slide the cursor down the Add or Remove Buttons menu, and the entire Picture Toolbar menu appears with a check box next to each icon. Deselect a check box to remove an item from the Picture Toolbar.

Auto Thumbnails

An *Auto Thumbnail* is a handy tool that enables you to create a mini-version of a picture. This is particularly useful when you want to use an image as a button that then links to a larger version of the picture. To create an Auto Thumbnail, click the Auto Thumbnail button on the Picture Toolbar after you select an image.

When you create a thumbnail and go to save the page, FrontPage prompts you to save the new thumbnail image that you created. After you load the page in a browser, you see the thumbnail rather than the original image. Then, when you click the thumbnail, the larger version appears in the Web browser by itself.

To specify your Auto Thumbnail preferences, follow these steps:

1. Choose Tools⇨Page Options from the menu bar to open the Page Options dialog box.

2. Click the AutoThumbnail tab.

3. Set your pixel sizes and border options. You can use three basic options to change the appearance of the thumbnails:

- **Thumbnail Size:** To set the size of the thumbnail, choose one of the four sizing options from the drop-down list and then enter the size (in pixels) that you want the thumbnail to be.

- **Borders:** By selecting the Border Thickness check box, you can include a border around your thumbnail. When you check the box, the Pixels field becomes available. In this field, enter the width (in pixels) that you want the border to be.

- **Bevel:** When you select this check box, FrontPage bevels the edges of the thumbnail.

4. Click OK. FrontPage changes your Auto Thumbnail preferences.

Beveling an Image

Beveling adds both a border and three-dimensional depth to a graphic. More often than not, you bevel an image to create a button effect. Follow these easy steps to bevel an image in FrontPage 2000:

1. In the Normal View, click the image that you want to bevel.

 2. Click the Bevel button on the Picture Toolbar. The button adds a bevel to your graphic, as shown in the following figure.

3. If you want to make the bevel darker and add more emphasis to it, click the Bevel button again.

Brightness and Contrast

Changing a graphic's *brightness* makes the graphic appear lighter or darker. Changing a graphic's *contrast* makes the graphic's individual pixels either stand out more or become more muted. Usually, setting a graphic's contrast goes hand in hand with changing the graphic's brightness. So, for example, the brighter a graphic becomes, the more contrast you need to avoid it becoming washed out.

To modify brightness and contrast for a graphic in FrontPage 2000, follow these steps:

1. In the Normal View, click the image that you want to modify.

2. Click any of the four Contrast or Brightness options on the Picture Toolbar:

- **More Contrast** increases the color distinctions between pixels.

- **Less Contrast** makes the colors blend together.

- **More Brightness** washes the image out.

- **Less Brightness** darkens the image.

Every time you click a button, the brightness or contrast either increases or decreases incrementally. The more times you click the More Brightness button, for example, the brighter the image gets.

You can undo your work by pressing Ctrl+Z. In fact, FrontPage supports multiple undos, so if you're fiddling with an image and you want to return it to its previous condition, press Ctrl+Z a few times.

Although they're a bit more extreme, two other ways to change brightness and contrast exist in FrontPage 2000. To completely wash out an image, click the image that you want to modify and then click the Wash Out button on the Picture Toolbar. It's a lot like throwing in too much bleach while washing your favorite printed T-shirt. To get rid of the color altogether, click the image and then click the Black and White button on the Picture Toolbar.

Cropping an Image

Cropping reduces an image in size. Cropping images comes in handy if, say, you have a picture of you and your mother-in-law and you want to eliminate your mother-in-law from the picture. To be honest, though, FrontPage's cropping features are limited in that you can crop only rectangular areas.

To crop an image in FrontPage, follow these steps:

1. Click the image that you want to crop.

2. Click the Crop button on the Picture Toolbar. After you click the button, a rectangular box appears inside the image's border, as shown in the following figure.

3. Click the anchor points and move the rectangle around if you want to resize the cropping area. You can also use the arrow keys to move the cropping area around the image after you've created it.

4. Press Enter to crop the image to the size of the rectangle.

Remember: Cropping cuts away everything that remains outside the cropping rectangle. If you specify an area, you're specifying the area of the image that you want to keep, not the area that you want to cut.

If you decide that you don't want to crop an image, press the Escape key to disengage the cropping tool.

WARNING

After you click the Crop button, you can't deselect the tool by clicking the button again. Clicking the Crop button a second time crops the image to the size of the rectangle. You must press Esc to deselect the cropping tool.

Flipping and Rotating Images

FrontPage makes flipping and rotating images easy. Here are the steps:

1. Click the graphic that you want to flip or rotate.

2. Click the Rotate Left, Rotate Right, Flip Horizontal, or Flip Vertical button on the Picture Toolbar, depending on the action that you want to initiate. You have the following two options with each button:

 • **Rotate Left** rotates the image 90 degrees to the left.

 • **Rotate Right** rotates the image 90 degrees to the right.

 • **Flip Horizontal** mirrors the image left to right.

 • **Flip Vertical** mirrors the image top to bottom.

Hyperlinking to an Image

Using images as hyperlinks can add pizzazz and flair to a Web site. Follow these steps to add a hyperlink to an image:

1. In the Normal View, click the image that you want to make a hyperlink.

2. Choose Insert⇨Hyperlink from the menu bar or press Ctrl+K. The Create Hyperlink dialog box that appears may look familiar; it's the same dialog box that FrontPage uses to create text hyperlinks.

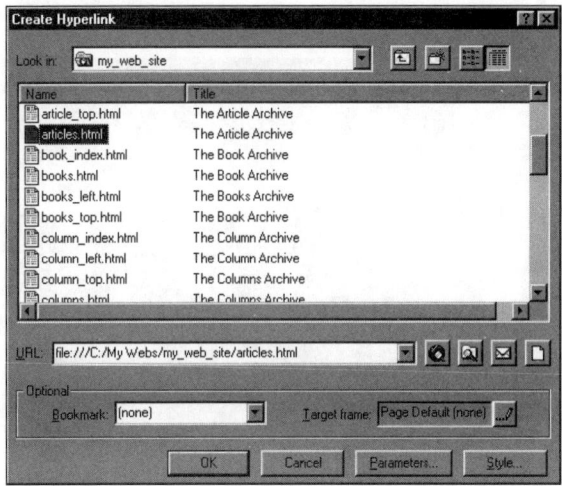

See Part IV for more information about creating text hyperlinks.

You can also create a link by selecting an object in the Normal View and then clicking the Hyperlink button on the Standard Toolbar.

3. Type the URL that you want the image to link to in the URL text box.

In addition to other Web pages, you can link to other graphics files from a hyperlink. For example, if you have a large picture that you want to show off, you can add a link to a thumbnail image of the picture that loads the larger image. The capability to use thumbnail images as links to larger images keeps your page size down and makes including other elements on the page easier.

4. Click OK. You can now use the image as a hyperlink on your Web page.

Image Maps

Image maps are great navigation tools that you see in many Web sites. You load a Web page, and a big graphic appears smack dab in the middle of the page. On the graphic are a host of hot links to various locations. How did the Web designers create such a helpful tool, you ask? The answer lies in image maps.

Image map

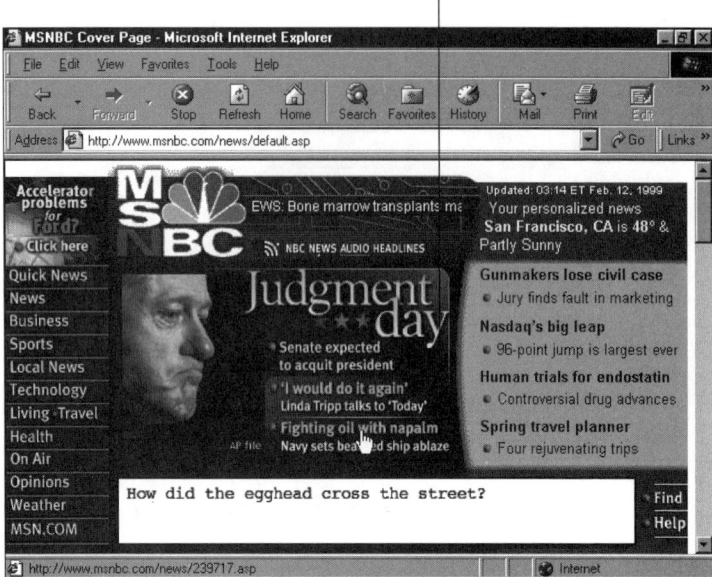

You create image maps by specifying regions of a graphic and then setting links for those regions. In the past, you had to create image maps in a separate program and then load the maps into your Web page. Times change, however. The following steps show you how to create an image map in FrontPage:

1. In the Normal View, click the graphic for which you want to create an image map.

2. Select one of the image map shape tools from the Picture Toolbar. FrontPage provides the following three shape tools for creating image maps:

- **Rectangular Hotspots** creates squares and rectangles. To create a square or rectangular link, click the image and then drag the mouse while holding down the mouse button. A square image is created from the point at which you first clicked.

- **Circular Hotspots** creates circles and ovals. You create a circular link precisely like you do a rectangular hotspot.

- **Polygonal Hotspots** enables you to create multisided polygon areas. Click the image once to create a path, and click again to specify the points for the linked area. You finish creating the polygon by selecting the first path point.

3. Create the shape that you want as a link by using one of the tools just listed. After you create the shape, the Create Hyperlink dialog box appears.

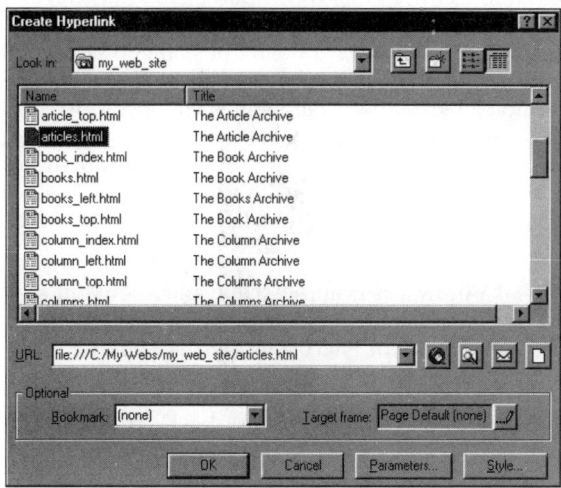

4. Type the link in the URL text box. Alternatively, you can use the drop-down list in the Create Hyperlink dialog box to search for other pages within your Web to link to. (*See also* "Creating and Using Hyperlinks" in Part IV.)

5. Click OK to set the hyperlink.

 You may want to move your link around on the graphic after you create it. To do so, click the arrow button on the Picture Toolbar and then click and hold down on the hotspot. As long as you hold down the mouse button, you can drag the hotspot around on the graphic.

 To change the size of the link, click and hold down on any of the link's *anchor points* — the square dots along the outline of the link area. Then drag the anchor to the desired location, and FrontPage automatically scales the link according to where you moved the anchor point. Letting go of the mouse button changes the link's size.

Moving Images Forward and Backward

If you have two images that you positioned absolutely (*see also* the section "Positioning an Image Absolutely," later in this part) and they overlap, how do you decide which image goes on top and which one goes on the bottom? A dilemma? Not really. Stealing a page right out the Microsoft Word play book, FrontPage 2000 enables you to establish layer relationships

between images so that you can place overlapping images on top of one another in the order you choose.

Although the idea of moving an image forward or backward may be common to Word and PowerPoint users, the concept's very new to the world of Web publishing. That's because moving an image forward or backward wasn't possible in Web publishing until the advent of Cascading Style Sheets (CSS). CSS includes a command called z-index that enables you to set objects in layers. Objects with the same z-index are in the same layer and can't overlap one another, while those with a z-index of –1, for example, are in the layer behind those with a z-index of 0. The default layer for standard HTML objects (tables, paragraph tags, and so on) is a z-index value of 0.

Only the 4.*x* browsers from Netscape and Microsoft support Cascading Style Sheets. If you're using an earlier version of either Netscape Navigator or Microsoft Internet Explorer, the browser will simply ignore the Cascading Style Sheets.

To move an image either forward or backward, follow these steps:

1. Click the graphic that you want to move.

2. Click either the Bring Forward button to move the image forward or the Send Backward button to move the image backward. The more times you click these buttons, the farther forward or backward the image moves. So if you click Send Backward five times, the image ends up five layers below an image that you don't move.

3. If you want to double-check that your image did in fact move forward or backward, move the image around on-screen. You'll notice that — depending on which button you clicked — the image moves over other pieces of text or slips behind them.

See "Cascading Style Sheets" in Part VII to find out how to set the z-index for text elements.

Placing Text over an Image

If you wanted to go through the trouble of creating a text layer and using Cascading Style Sheets to put the text layer over an image, you could; but doing so would be a little bit like shooting ants with an elephant gun. Alternatively, FrontPage 2000 supports a clever little way of placing text in image maps to achieve the same effect.

What do you have to do? Just follow these steps:

1. Click the graphic over which you want to place text.

2. Click the Text button on the Picture Toolbar. Doing so generates a text box in the middle of your graphic. To resize the text box, drag the box's anchor points with your cursor.

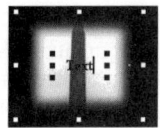

3. Type the text that you want in the text box.

4. Press Escape to deselect the text box.

To generate another text box on that image, simply click the Text button again. If you want to move a text box around on the image, click and hold down the mouse button while the cursor is in the middle of the text box and then move the text box to its new location.

Because this graphic is essentially an image map with text, you can also turn these text boxes into hyperlinks. Just press Ctrl+K to open the Edit Hyperlink dialog box after you create a text box on a selected image. Then enter the link location and click OK to add the link to the text on the image. (*See also* "Creating and Using Hyperlinks" in Part IV.)

If you're using other image types in your Web page — a .jpg image, for example — FrontPage tries to turn the image into a .gif file when you click the Text button on the Picture Toolbar. In most cases, this compromises the graphical quality of the image you're adding text to, because converting from a .jpg to a .gif reduces the number of colors in the image.

Positioning an Image Absolutely

Absolute positioning enables Web developers to place or move an image to any location on-screen, regardless of whether that image is part of a table or any other page element.

To do absolute positioning, FrontPage uses Cascading Style Sheets, which are not supported in the older 3.*x* browsers. *See* Part VII for more information about Cascading Style Sheets and how they're used in FrontPage 2000.

To position an image absolutely, follow these steps:

1. In the Normal View, click the image that you want to position absolutely.

2. Click the Position Absolutely button on the Picture Toolbar.

3. Click and drag the image to the desired location on-screen.

Scaling an Image

Scaling, unlike cropping, is the process of making an entire image either larger or smaller. There's no cutting away of the image involved here. In fact, there isn't even a button for this one! You can scale an image just by clicking the image.

After you click an image, you see anchor points appear around the image's border. To scale the image, click and drag one of these anchor points. The image resizes itself according to where you let go of the anchor point.

 To scale an image and keep its proportions intact, choose one of the corner anchor points and then scale the image. Scaling in this manner keeps the *aspect ratio* (the height-to-width ratio of the image) consistent as the image gets bigger or smaller.

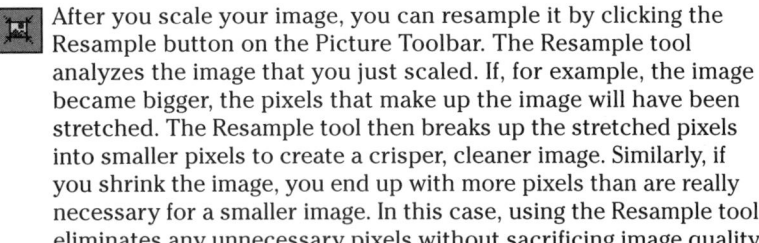 After you scale your image, you can resample it by clicking the Resample button on the Picture Toolbar. The Resample tool analyzes the image that you just scaled. If, for example, the image became bigger, the pixels that make up the image will have been stretched. The Resample tool then breaks up the stretched pixels into smaller pixels to create a crisper, cleaner image. Similarly, if you shrink the image, you end up with more pixels than are really necessary for a smaller image. In this case, using the Resample tool eliminates any unnecessary pixels without sacrificing image quality.

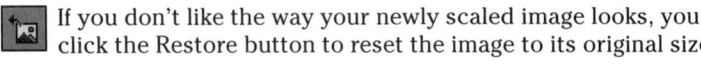 If you don't like the way your newly scaled image looks, you can click the Restore button to reset the image to its original size.

 You can use the Restore button on a number of other Picture Toolbar features as well, including the Color, Brightness, Contrast, Rotate, and Flip tools.

Scanning an Image

To scan an image into FrontPage 2000, you must first have a scanner. Then follow these steps:

1. Choose Insert⇨Picture⇨From File from the menu bar. The Picture dialog box appears.

2. Click the Scan button in the bottom-right corner of the Picture dialog box. Doing so brings up the Camera/Scanner dialog box. Make sure that your scanner is plugged in and turned on and that you have an image to scan in the scanner.

3. Click the Source button to specify your scanner. In the Select Source dialog box that appears, select from the available scanners on your system and then click the Select button.

4. Click the Acquire button to scan the image and add it to your Web page.

Setting an Image's Transparent Color

Gif images support transparency, which means that you can choose to make a particular color on your image invisible. This feature is downright helpful if you have a square graphic and you want to display only the logo in the middle of the image. With FrontPage 2000, setting the transparent color is a cinch! Here's what you do:

1. Click the graphic that contains the color you want to make transparent.

2. Click the Set Transparent Color button on the Picture Toolbar.

3. Click the color on the image that you want to make transparent. After you do so, all instances of that color in the image become invisible, and you can see the Web page background through it.

Choose a color for the transparency that you're not likely to need from the Web palette. Gray, lime green, and hot pink are all good choices for the transparent color. (You choose the transparent color as you edit the image in an image editor.)

If you're using other image types in your Web page — a .jpg image, for example — FrontPage will try to turn the image into a .gif file when you click the Set Transparent Color button on the Picture Toolbar. In addition, you can set only one transparent color with this tool. If you select the tool again and click another color, that color becomes the transparent color, and the preceding transparent color is no longer transparent.

Part VI

Using FrontPage 2000 with Office 2000

With Office 2000, Microsoft made a fundamental change in the way documents are created and maintained, choosing to use HTML as the foundation for all documents created throughout the new Office suite. This part covers the new features in FrontPage 2000 that support this new level of interoperability.

In this part . . .

✔ Using add-ins

✔ Connecting a Microsoft Access database to a Web

✔ Importing Office files

✔ Inserting an Office spreadsheet

✔ Importing tables and charts

✔ Working with object programming tools

✔ Using Outlook to send Webs and Web pages

Add-Ins

Add-ins are just like they sound. They're programs (that are developed either by Microsoft or by third parties) that add functionality to a copy of FrontPage 2000.

For the latest information about available add-ins for FrontPage 2000, you can visit the Microsoft Office Update Web site at `officeupdate.microsoft.com/default.htm`.

To load an add-in into FrontPage, follow these steps:

1. Choose Tools⇨Add-ins from the menu bar.

2. In the COM Add-ins dialog box that appears, click Add to search for a new add-in.

3. Select the add-in that you want and then click OK to load the add-in.

Connecting a Microsoft Access Database to a Web

Adding a Microsoft Access database adds powerful functionality to your Web site. With a database, you can do everything from simply displaying different kinds of data — say, client contact information — to creating entire Web pages directly from the information stored in the database.

Although designing databases is a tad bit beyond the scope of this book, connecting databases to your FrontPage Web certainly is not! To connect an Access database to your Web and display data from it, follow these steps:

1. Bring the Access database (an .mdb file) into your Web.

You import a Microsoft Access database into your Web in the same way that you would import any other kind of file. The easiest way is to drag the .mdb file from your hard drive (or the network) into the Folder List while either the Page View or the Folders View is activated.

Alternatively, you can import an .mdb file by choosing File⇨Import and clicking the Add File button in the Import dialog box that appears.

2. From the Add File to Import List dialog box that appears, select a database from either your local drive or a network drive; then click Open to add the file to your Import list. Then click OK to import the file.

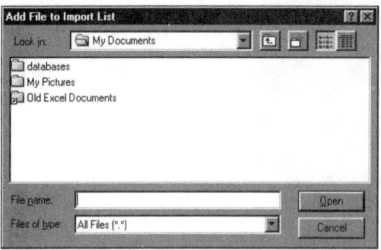

3. Choose Insert⇨Database⇨Results from the menu bar. This action brings up the Database Results Wizard dialog box. You have three options for adding a database to your Web:

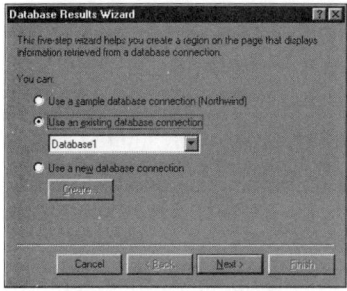

- **Use a Sample Database Connection:** FrontPage 2000 comes with a sample database that you can use to get a feel for how a database in a Web works. The database, from the fictional Northwind, includes a number of different categories of data, including customer information, products, and suppliers, all of which can be accessed in the Web.

- **Use an Existing Database Connection:** If you've previously added a database to your Web and added a connection to it, you can choose it from this drop-down list.

- **Use a New Database Connection:** If you want to use a database that is in your Web but is not yet connected, choose this option. When you click the Create button, the Web Settings dialog box appears with the Database tab selected.

  See Part III for details on how to add a database connection in FrontPage 2000.

4. Click Next.

5. Select a record source or create a custom query. FrontPage provides two ways to get data from a database:

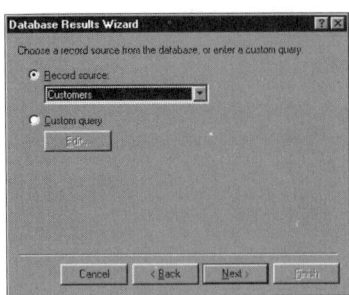

- Select a table from the database and display the records that fit that category. This is the simpler way of displaying database records, and the one I follow in this example.

- Ask the database for information. Using the Structured Query Language (SQL), you can use HTML forms to pass along parameters to a database and then have it return only the records you need. This is a vastly more complex method, one for which FrontPage offers only limited support.

For more information about getting started with SQL, check out *SQL For Dummies* by Allen G. Taylor (published by IDG Books Worldwide, Inc.).

However, if you're already familiar with creating SQL queries, then the Custom Query radio button may be the route for you. Select it to get the Custom Query dialog box, where you can input an SQL query to pass through to the database.

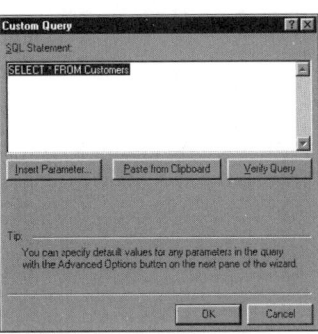

6. Click Next.

7. Verify your fields. FrontPage checks the database for the fields within the record type you selected. It then displays those fields in the Displayed Fields list.

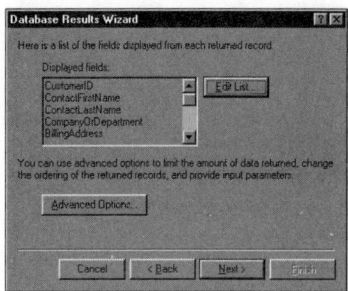

You can edit the fields that will be displayed in the Web page by clicking the Edit List button. From the Displayed Fields dialog box, you can add and remove fields, as well as change the order in which the fields will be displayed in the Web page. After you complete this step, click OK to return to the Database Results Wizard.

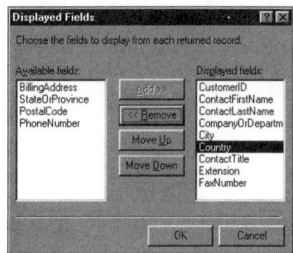

If you want to limit the number of records that are displayed from the database, click the Advanced Options button. From the Advanced Options dialog box, you can

• Click the Criteria button to choose from a fixed set of criteria that serve to limit the number of records returned from the database.

• Click the Ordering button to sort the records that are returned from the database.

• Select the Limit the Number of Returned Records to display a fixed number of records.

• Specify the message that is displayed when no records are returned from the database by typing that message in the Message to Display if No Records Are Returned box.

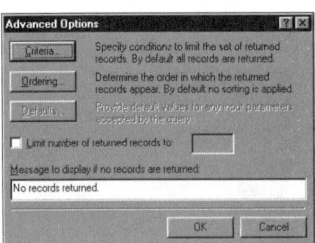

8. After you set your options for limiting your database results, click OK to return to the Database Results Wizard.

9. Click Next to select your layout options. Here, you can specify the way in which the data is organized within the Web page. In the drop-down list box, you can choose to view the data in table format or as a list.

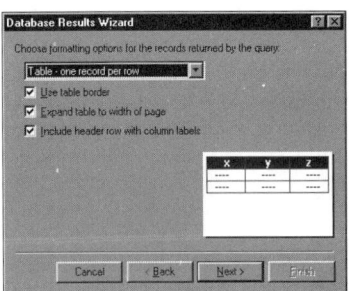

10. Click Next to select whether the data is displayed all together in groupings or as a single item.

Here, you have two options: Display All Records Together and Split Records into Groups. If you select the latter radio button, you can also enter the number of records you want in each group in the Records Per Group field.

11. Click Finish to generate the database. A sample end result appears in the following figure.

If you're working locally on your machine (as opposed to creating the database connection on a FrontPage server), you'll get the following message when you finish creating the database connection:

```
This is the start of a Database Results region.
The region will not work unless the page has a
file extension of ".asp". The page must be
fetched from a Web server with a Web browser to
display correctly; the current Web is stored on
your local disk or network.
```

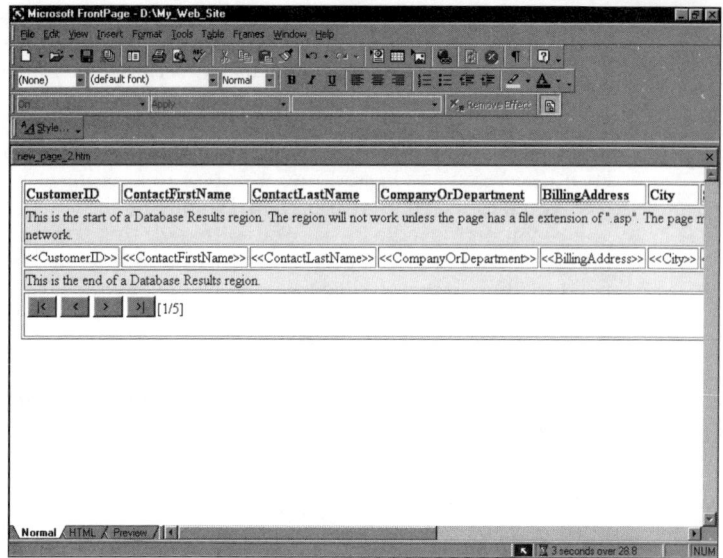

12. To save your Web page as an .asp file, choose File⇨Save As
from the menu bar and then choose Active Server Page (*.asp)
from the drop-down list. Then click OK to save the page. When
you then post the page to a FrontPage server, the results will
appear correctly.

Check out *FrontPage 2000 For Dummies* (IDG Books Worldwide) for
more information about database publishing.

Importing Office Files

With Office 2000, Microsoft has completely overhauled its file
formats for Office documents. Why is this important, you ask?
Well, because the standard Office file format is now HTML, it
should, in theory, be easier to exchange documents among Office
products, including FrontPage 2000.

In practical terms, there are two levels to this interoperability:

+ **Converting files from their native file format — say, an
Excel spreadsheet (.xls) — to HTML:** Although the file
formats may be native HTML in FrontPage 2000, this functionality was available in previous versions of FrontPage, as well
as in Excel, Word, and PowerPoint. In other words, this
change is no big deal.

✦ **Embedding Office objects, such as editable spreadsheets and pivot charts, into the actual HTML files:** This is the level of interoperability that I discuss in various sections later in this part.

Remember: Importing generally means one of two things in FrontPage: You can import into a Web or import into the HTML file that you happen to be working on. When you choose File➪Import, you're importing a file into a Web. Although this step brings a file into your Web, it doesn't automatically put it in your Web. You need to choose Insert➪File to embed a file in your HTML page.

Inserting a Word 2000 file into a Web page

To insert a Word 2000 document directly into a Web page, follow these steps:

1. Choose Insert➪File from the menu bar. The Select File dialog box appears.

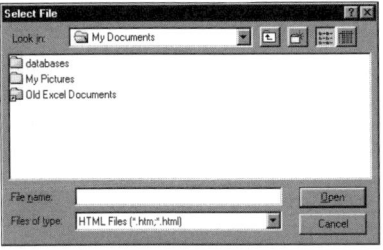

2. Choose the kind of Word file that you want to import from the available choices in the Files of Type drop-down list.

FrontPage allows you to choose from nearly all the previous versions of Microsoft Word, as well as rich text format and several other word-processing programs.

3. Search for the file you want to import on your local or network drive through the Look In menu.

4. Click Open to insert the file into your Web page.

Note: FrontPage 2000 dynamically converts the file to HTML and maintains the basic layout of the document. It does not, however, embed the document properties into the HTML. As a result, things such as automated fields for date entry into a document will not carry over into the HTML version of the document.

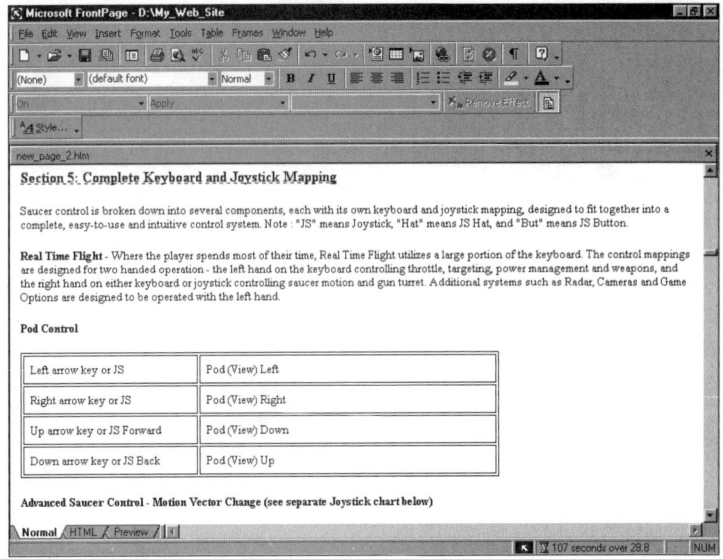

Although Office 2000 now uses HTML as the underpinning for all document types, don't be surprised when you insert a Word file into a Web page and it looks markedly different than it does in Word. Although using HTML as a document format may enable easier file translation, FrontPage is still trying to replicate the physical structure and display it on-screen by using a different set of tools. This attempt inevitably results in variations between the Word file and the HTML translation you see in FrontPage.

Importing an Excel spreadsheet into a Web page

For the most part, importing an Excel 2000 spreadsheet works exactly the same way as importing a Word document. The same rules about document functionality being disabled apply here. As a result, when you import an Excel spreadsheet, you're really taking all the data from the spreadsheet cells and converting it to a text table. After this data is in FrontPage, it is just values; all the formulas are gone.

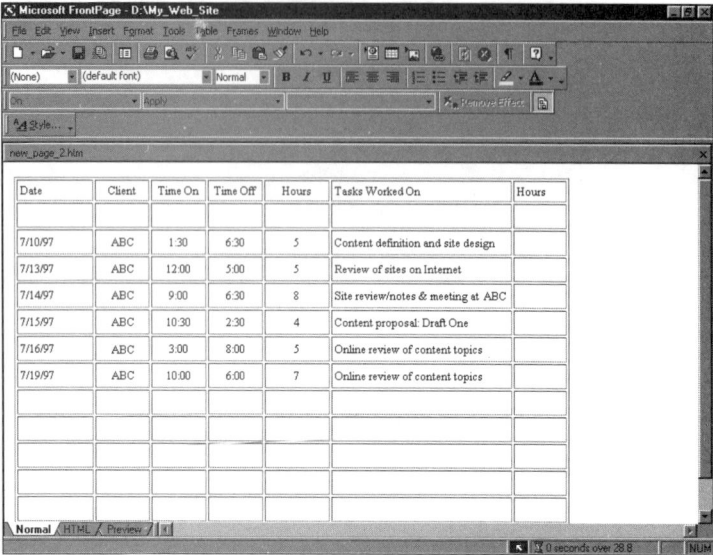

This doesn't mean that you can't have editable Excel spreadsheet cells in FrontPage. *See* "Inserting an Office Spreadsheet" later in this part for the lowdown on this technique.

Importing a PowerPoint presentation into a Web page

PowerPoint 2000 represents perhaps the strangest implementation of an Office document into FrontPage. In PowerPoint, you can convert a presentation into HTML. PowerPoint generates all the graphics and HTML for you there. From there, you can then import the Office document into FrontPage the same way you'd import any other folder's worth of data.

Importing a PowerPoint presentation directly into FrontPage before converting it to HTML, however, is a more complex proposition. Unlike Word and Excel files, you can't use the Insert⊏>File route that I described earlier. Rather, you have to import the presentation file (.ppt) into your Web first. Do so by following these steps:

1. Choose File⊏>Import to bring up the Import dialog box.

2. In the Import dialog box, click the Add File button.

3. Select Microsoft Office Files from the Files of Type drop-down list.

4. On your local or network drive, find the PowerPoint presentation that you want to import. Click the file that you want to import, and then click the Open button.

5. In the Import dialog box, click OK to insert the presentation into your Web page.

After you've brought the PowerPoint presentation into your Web, you can link to it from your Web page. The easiest way to create this link is to drag the presentation from the Folder List into your Web page. FrontPage automatically generates a hyperlink to the file.

Note to Internet Explorer users: When you select the link, the presentation is loaded in the browser window, and you can scroll down through the entire presentation.

This embedding of the presentation works only in Internet Explorer Version 4.0 or higher. If you're using Netscape Navigator, the link simply prompts a download of the file and then the activation of PowerPoint in its regular manner. There's no integration with the Web browser at all.

In addition, a number of PowerPoint specific controls become available to Web viewers, including

♦ **Advance and reverse buttons for the slide show**

♦ **Print, copy, and edit features of PowerPoint:** That's right: You can edit the PowerPoint presentation live within your Web browser, as long as you have PowerPoint 2000 installed on your machine. The PowerPoint interface replaces the standard Web browser rendering window and file structure, and you can edit the slide content just as if you were working in PowerPoint 2000.

♦ **Full-screen viewing of the presentation:** If you choose this option, the Internet Explorer interface disappears, and the presentation takes over the entire screen. In this case, a floating navigation menu appears in the bottom-left corner of the presentation so that you can move your way through it.

For more information about how PowerPoint 2000 works with Internet Explorer and Windows, check out *PowerPoint 2000 For Windows For Dummies* by Doug Lowe (published by IDG Books Worldwide, Inc.).

Inserting an Office Chart

An Office chart is much like the charting function in Excel — so much so, in fact, that it won't work in FrontPage unless you have a data source in your Web page from which to gather data. Put another way, if you're going to insert an Office chart, you'd better already have an Office spreadsheet embedded in the Web page, too.

After you have a data source in your Web page, you can generate an Office chart by following these steps:

1. Choose Insert⇨Component⇨Office Chart from the menu bar. If you have a data source in the page, the Chart Wizard appears to guide you through the chart generation process.

   If you don't have a data source selected, FrontPage prompts you that there's no data source in the page and that, therefore, the wizard can't start. It then embeds an empty graph in your Web page!

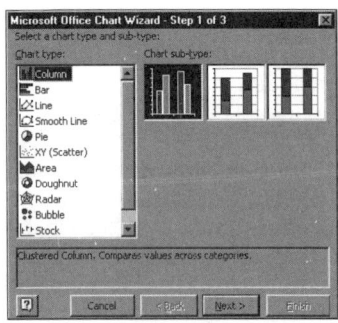

If you abort the Wizard, FrontPage generates an empty graph for your Web page. If you want to restart the wizard, you need to bring up the Office Chart Properties Toolbox by right-clicking one of the cells and choosing Property Toolbox from the pop-up menu. Then select the General tab and click the chart icon.

2. Click the Chart Type and Chart Sub-Type that you want for the data on the Web page, and then click the Next button.

3. Specify your data source. This may sound odd given that you can't even use the wizard if you don't have a data source in the page, but here's the rationale: If you have a database providing data, as well as, say, an Office spreadsheet, you need a way to choose between them in the wizard. So, in this step, FrontPage scans your Web page for data sources and then lists them for you. Click the source you want to use, and then click Next to continue.

4. Specify the table settings. Depending on the types of data you have available and the cells you have selected, FrontPage tries to figure out your table options for you. However, you have total control to set it up any way you like. From this dialog box, you can do the following:

- Create or delete a *series,* which is just a set of values with a label. FrontPage tries to do this for you, creating a "default" series that includes any data you've highlighted in your Office spreadsheet, but you can also do it yourself. To add a series, click the Add button. In the Name field, type a name for the series, and in the Value field, specify a data range based on the data source from which you're creating the graph. To specify the data range, you use standard Excel formula syntax.

For more information about Excel formula syntax, check out *Excel 2000 For Dummies* by Greg Harvey (published by IDG Books Worldwide, Inc.).

- Assign category labels to the graph from the Office Spreadsheet data source. In the Category (X) Axis Labels field, use the same Excel formula syntax to specify which cells in the Office spreadsheet you want to serve as labels in your graph.

After you're done setting your graph parameters, click the Finish button to insert the graph into your Web page.

Like the other components, an Office chart also has a Property Toolbox. From that toolbox, you can

✦ Change the chart type.

✦ Edit the plot area configuration.

✦ Undo your work and access the Chart help.

Inserting an Office Pivot Table

Note: This section covers only cursorily the Pivot Table feature within FrontPage 2000. Check out the big brother to this book, *FrontPage 2000 For Dummies,* for a more complete and thorough discussion of how Pivot Tables work and how to get one up and running in your FrontPage Web.

What an Office spreadsheet is to Excel 2000, an Office Pivot Table is to Microsoft Access 2000. In short, a Pivot Table enables users to view summary data from a database file and not only display it but also edit that data and generate reports from it.

For a good primer on the features of Microsoft Access and how you can best utilize them by using the Pivot Tables in FrontPage 2000, check out *Access 2000 For Windows For Dummies* by John Kaufeld (published by IDG Books Worldwide, Inc.).

Like the Office spreadsheet feature, the Pivot Table feature is available only in Internet Explorer 4.0 or higher browsers. Additionally, it's really only valuable if you constantly use databases as part of your daily business.

Essentially, there are four steps to activating a Pivot Table:

1. Choose Insert⇨Component⇨Office Pivot Table to embed an empty Pivot Table in your Web page. This is the easy part.

2. Activate the PivotTable Property Toolbox by right-clicking one of the cells and choosing Property Toolbox from the pop-up menu.

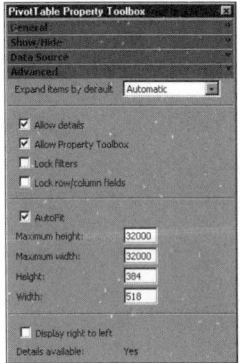

3. Link to a data source. The Pivot Table requires that you link to an SQL server database in order to query the data that you're going to use for summary reports. You set these preferences clicking the Data Source tab in the PivotTable Property Toolbox.

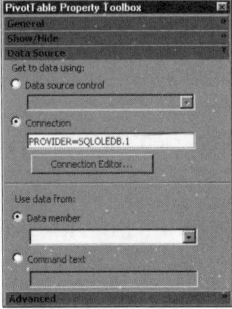

It's good to know that when linking to this data source, FrontPage provides a host of log-on and password protection options. You get the following dialog box when you click the Connection Editor button in the Data Source tab of the PivotTable Property Toolbox.

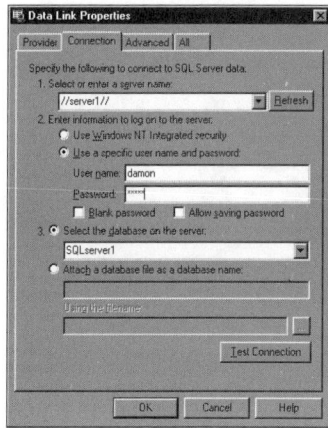

4. Create summary fields in the Pivot Table by dragging items from the Field List.

You may need to activate the Field List first. To do so, right-click one of the cells and choose Field List from the pop-up menu.

After you've connected to a data source, the available fields appear in the Pivot Table Field List window. You can then generate a summary report from a field by dragging that field name from the List into the Pivot Table window in the HTML file.

Inserting an Office Spreadsheet

I can see that strange look on your face from here. So what's the difference between importing an Excel spreadsheet (see the preceding section) and inserting an Office spreadsheet? Actually, the difference is night and day. Importing an Excel spreadsheet merely converts cell content into a table, but inserting an Office spreadsheet embeds a fully functioning Excel-like editable spreadsheet document into your Web page.

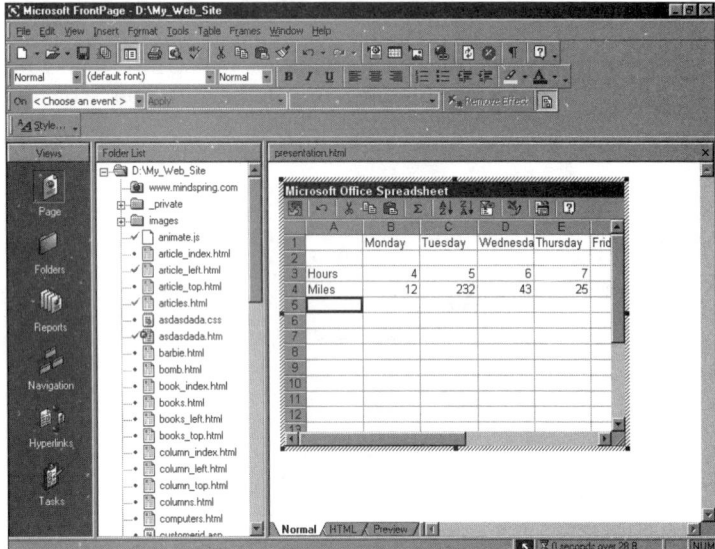

Note: Microsoft is able to achieve this rather dramatic feat by using its ActiveX controls to embed spreadsheets. Now, as you may expect, this feature works exceptionally well with Internet Explorer 4.0 and higher, but it doesn't work at all with Netscape Navigator.

Unlike an embedded PowerPoint presentation, which seems to take over the entire browser, an Office spreadsheet is decidedly understated. To embed a spreadsheet, choose Insert⇨Component⇨ Office Spreadsheet.

When the spreadsheet first comes up in FrontPage, you'll be hard pressed to find a toolbar associated with it. To activate the toolbar for the spreadsheet, right-click one of the cells and choose Property Toolbox from the pop-up menu. The Spreadsheet Property Toolbox lets you work with the following items:

✦ General tools such as Undo and Help

✦ Text-formatting tools

✦ Show and Hide preferences for the spreadsheet

✦ Cell calculation preferences

✦ A Find File tool

✦ A data importing tool

✦ Cell protection and locking

✦ Title bar preferences

✦ Advanced preferences such as scroll bars and maximum cell heights

 To resize your spreadsheet (they're kind of small when you first import them), click and drag one of the anchor points surrounding the spreadsheet object in the Normal View.

Object Programming Tools

FrontPage 2000 comes with a powerful suite of tools that enable you to build powerful applets and feature modifications to FrontPage itself. These scripting tools are common among all Office applications. In FrontPage, you have three tools to choose from:

✦ **Macros:** A macro is essentially a set of automated tasks that FrontPage does for you. A macros can be anything from a simple replication of keystrokes to the calculation and insertion of data or text. To create a macro, choose Tools⇨ Macro⇨Macros. Enter a name in the Macro Name box and then click the Create button to generate the macro in the Visual Basic Editor.

✦ **Visual Basic Editing:** Visual Basic is far more powerful than macros are. Using Visual Basic, you can build application components tailored to your specific kinds of projects and use them in FrontPage. So, for example, if you want to create an automated template Web site that you can generate simply by filling out some basic data forms, the Visual Basic Editor is the place to generate that level of automation and functionality.

You can access the Visual Basic Editor by choosing Tools⇨ Macro⇨Visual Basic Editor.

✦ **Microsoft Script Editing:** The Microsoft Script Editor is an integrated tool that combines both HTML editing and in-depth programming tools. It enables you to edit HTML just like in the FrontPage editor, while also letting you build and compile scripts from other programming languages such as Visual Basic, Jscript, and Visual Basic Script (VBScript).

You can access the Microsoft Script Editor by choosing Tools⇨Macro⇨Microsoft Script Editor.

 For more information about object programming, check out *Object-Oriented Programming For Dummies* by Namir C. Shammas (published by IDG Books Worldwide, Inc.).

Sending Web Pages with Outlook

It's often helpful to send someone a Web page that you're working on to get that person's approval or feedback. If you're using Microsoft Outlook, doing so is quite easy with FrontPage. To send a Web page by using Microsoft Outlook, follow these steps:

1. Go to the page you want to send via e-mail.

2. Choose File⇨Send from the menu bar. Choosing this command activates Outlook and creates a blank message with the HTML attached to the message.

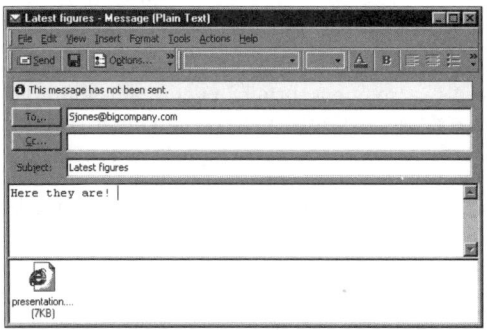

Technically, FrontPage launches your e-mail editor, no matter what it is. It doesn't have to be Outlook, but because this is Office 2000 and Outlook 2000 is a part of it, well, it seemed like a good place to start!

3. Fill in the e-mail address of the recipient in the To box, and be sure to include a subject in the Subject box.

4. Click Send to send the message with the attachment.

When you send an HTML page, you're sending only the HTML, not the graphics that come along with that page. When someone downloads it onto his or her machine, any graphics that are in the page aren't visible.

Part VII

Advanced Features in FrontPage 2000

The Web of the past was largely about HTML. The Web of today — and more important, the Web of tomorrow — is all about new technologies — things like Dynamic HTML and Cascading Style Sheets — and the applications that will come from them. This part highlights some of the exciting new things that you can do with the Web and your copy of FrontPage 2000.

In this part . . .

- ✔ ActiveX controls
- ✔ Forms
- ✔ Cascading Style Sheets
- ✔ Dynamic HTML
- ✔ Java applets
- ✔ Active Server pages

Adding ActiveX Controls

"What is ActiveX?" you may be wondering. That's a good question. Basically, *ActiveX* is Microsoft's attempt to merge the functionality of a Windows environment with a Web browser (and vice versa). Perhaps the most obvious example of this merger is the *Active Desktop,* which comes with the Internet Explorer 4.0 upgrade (if you're still using Windows 95), Windows 98, and Windows NT 4.0 and above.

The Active Desktop is a merging of the desktop and Internet Explorer. Folders on your desktop look just like mini-Internet Explorer windows. You can create links from your desktop to file locations or to sites out on the Internet. By using *Active Channels,* you can get Web content to stream directly to your desktop.

And these features are just the beginning, if Microsoft has anything to say about it (and it does). The big downside, as you might imagine, is that these ActiveX controls aren't part of either Mac or UNIX operating systems, nor are they a part of the Netscape Navigator browser. As a result, the only people to whom ActiveX means anything are Windows users with Internet Explorer 4.0 or above.

Those rather large and ominous caveats aside, you can embed a number of Windows-like tools in your Web pages, including the following:

 ✦ Microsoft direct animation tools

 ✦ Editable charts, table, graphs, and database items

 ✦ Toolbars

 ✦ Calendars

 ✦ Slider bars

For nearly all these objects, you need to write code to activate, deactivate, and otherwise use them. If you're not prepared to work with server-side XML or Java code, almost all these ActiveX objects will be of little or no value to you or your site.

To insert an ActiveX object in your Web page, follow these steps:

 1. Place your cursor where you want to insert the object and then choose Insert⇨Advanced⇨ActiveX Control from the menu bar. This action opens the Insert ActiveX Control dialog box, as shown in the following figure.

2. Select the ActiveX object that you want to insert into your Web page by clicking its name in the Select a Control list.

3. Click OK to insert the object.

Note: Beyond those listed in the ActiveX Control dialog box, a number of other ActiveX controls are available to FrontPage 2000 users. To activate these other controls, click the Customize button on the ActiveX Control dialog box to bring up the Customize ActiveX Control List dialog box. Click the check boxes next to the controls that you want to add to the ActiveX Control dialog box and then click OK.

Inserting ActiveX objects is just the beginning. You must tie them to an object, some code, or a file that contains data that you want to display (that is, a database).

To set the parameters for a given ActiveX object, double-click the object in the Normal View. For each object, you get an ActiveX Control Properties dialog box, much like the one shown in the following figure. In this dialog box, you specify the code and link it to the ActiveX control object.

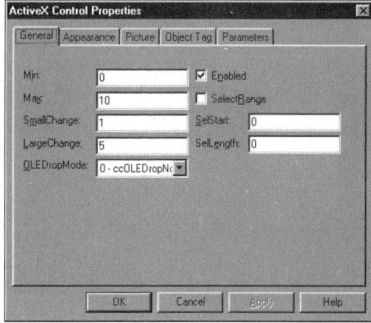

For a good primer on using XML and Java code in the creation of dynamic Web sites, as well as their interaction with the ActiveX controls, try jumping over to `www.builder.com` or `msdn.microsoft.com`. Other good sites to check out include `www.developer.com`, `www.webreference.com`, `www.perl.com`, and `www.xml.com`.

Building Forms

If you need forms, FrontPage 2000 comes with a number of options. Forms are the most common method for users of your Web site to interact with you or a database. A form looks just about how you'd imagine that it should. You create a series of fields into which users input information, and then they submit the form.

After a user submits a form, essentially, three things can happen:

✦ **The form interacts with a server.** You can use a form and post the results to a server a couple of different ways. You can simply send the data in the form to a text file, which then gets saved for future use. Alternatively, the form may interact with a database — say, to create a new user account or to request information from the database itself.

✦ **The form interacts with the HTML page itself.** Often, forms interact with JavaScript rather than with a server. This situation often involves cookies. Rather than posting the form to a server, the form queries some JavaScript in the HTML and then returns an answer based on the input.

✦ **The form interacts with the user's computer.** Sounds frightening, I know, but this happens all the time. Whether you're working from the local HTML or from a database on a server, form actions often result in the Web browser's placing a cookie on your computer. When this happens, the browser is writing a small text string — usually containing things such as your name and your e-mail address — in a specified location on your computer for retrieval by the Web browser at a later time.

 For more information about cookies and how they work, pick up a copy of *JavaScript For Dummies,* 2nd Edition, by Emily A. Vander Veer (published by IDG Books Worldwide, Inc.).

People use forms every day, so the fact that FrontPage 2000 comes with a robust set of tools for creating forms is no surprise at all.

Creating a simple form

Creating a form is the simple part. This stage is where you build the form's fields and buttons. The tough part comes later, when you need to actually send the data someplace! But that's putting the cart a bit in front of the horse.

To build a form, follow these steps:

1. Decide what kind of information you want to collect from each user. This step assumes that you've already answered the bigger question: "Why do I need to get information from the people coming to this Web site?" After you clear that hurdle, you usually find some common elements in forms, as the following list describes:

   • First and last name

   • Full address and telephone number

   • E-mail or Web site address

   • The product or service that interests the user

   • Feedback on how the user heard about the site or company

If you're doing e-commerce, the entire equation changes. You will use forms, but you're going to want to collect credit card numbers, process orders, and provide immediate feedback to potential buyers. This kind of form usage requires using the data security and encryption features built into the browsers, as well as a host of other Web tools that ensure that a user's credit card information can't be stolen by hackers or other prying eyes on the Internet.

2. Choose Insert⟹Form⟹Form from the menu bar. This action creates two buttons, as shown in the following figure. What you don't see, behind the scenes, is that FrontPage 2000 adds all the HTML you need to post your form and save the data in the form.

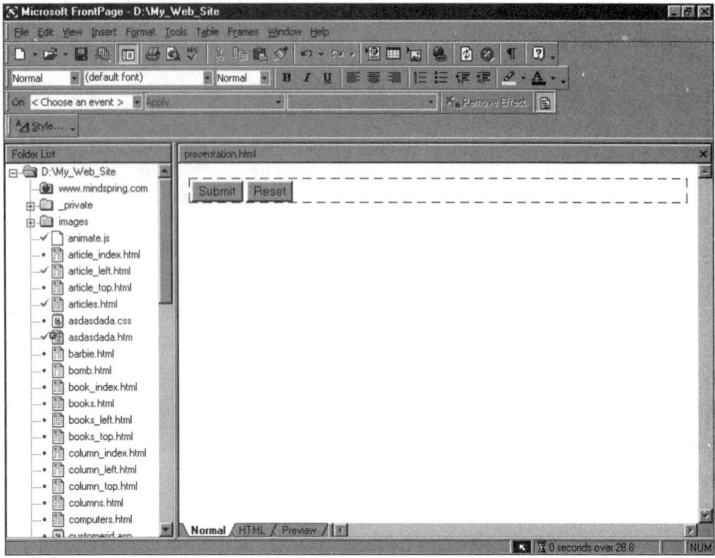

Adding fields, menus, and boxes to forms

So you've created the form — but if you don't have any fields in which to input data or menus from which to choose data, your form's not going to get you very far.

FrontPage 2000 provides seven different form fields to choose from. (Label isn't a form field; see the following section for more on labels.) You can insert the various field types into a form by following these steps:

1. In the Normal View, select the form in your Web page to which you want to add a field. You can do so by clicking and dragging across the form until it's highlighted.

2. Choose your desired location for the field by pressing Enter to move up or down within the form.

   Putting your fields above your Submit button usually makes the most sense. To do so, just make sure to place the cursor above the Submit button on the form and press Enter a couple of times to move the buttons down in the page.

3. Choose Insert⇨Form and then choose one of the seven form field types that you see on the Form submenu. The seven field types are all slightly different, and you use them in forms for different reasons. Briefly, here are the differences among them:

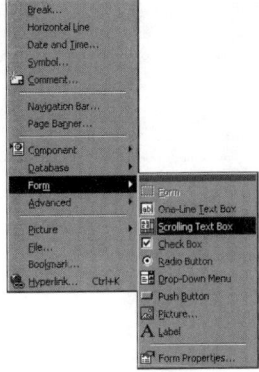

- **One-Line Text Box:** This kind of form field enables users to input text information directly into a field of a fixed size.

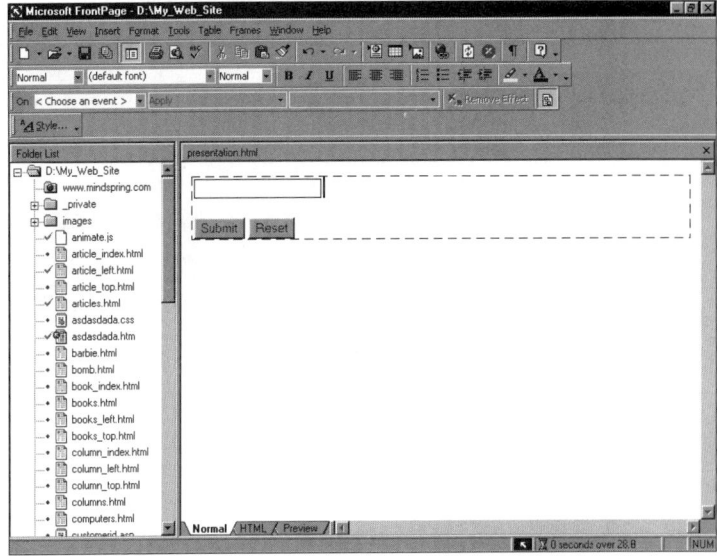

- **Scrolling Text Box:** This form field is similar to a one-line text box, except that it's larger and enables users to scroll down through the text they input.

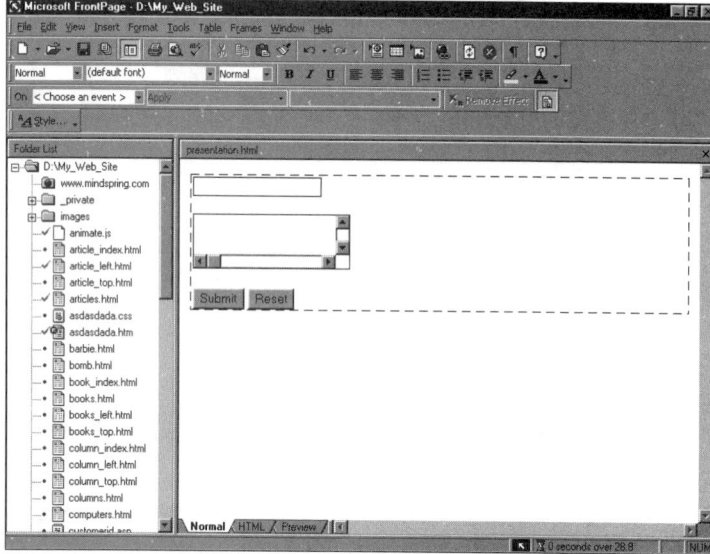

• **Check Box:** In creating a check box, you set a value for the box. When a user checks that box, the value gets sent when the form is submitted.

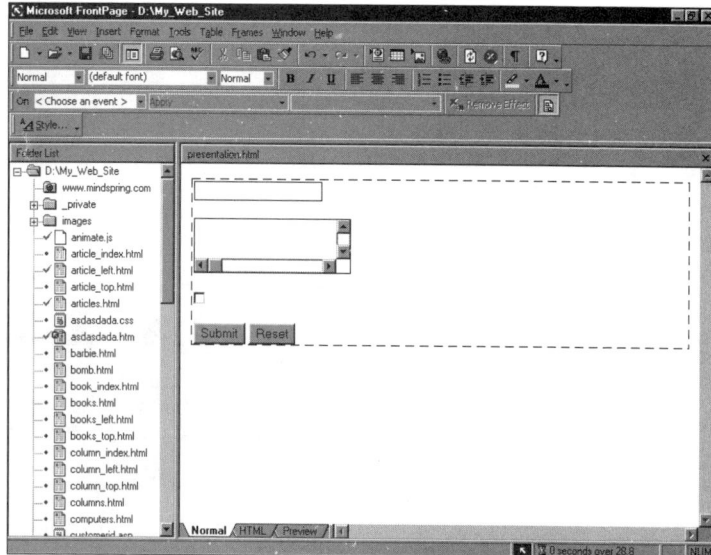

- **Radio Button:** A radio button works exactly like a check box, except that with radio buttons, you're allowed to select only one of the values in the list. (With check boxes, you can often select more than one value.)

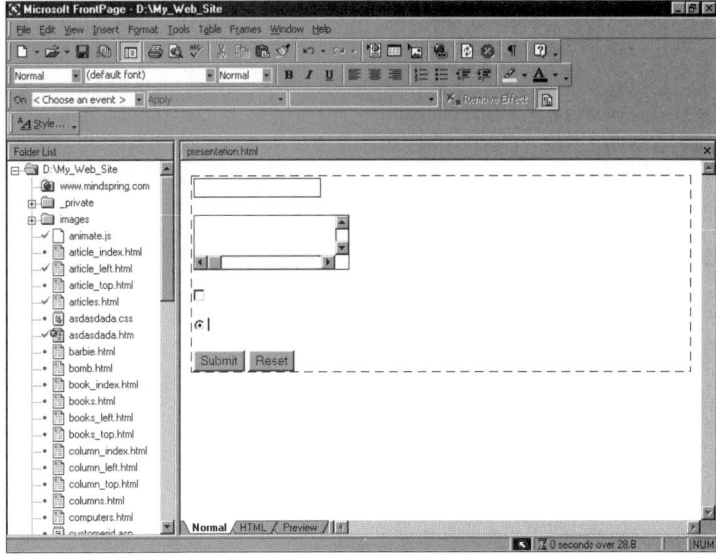

- **Drop-Down Menu:** A drop-down menu enables users to choose from a preset series of values by clicking the menu and dragging the cursor down until they highlight the value they want. (Let go of the cursor while a value is highlighted to select it.)

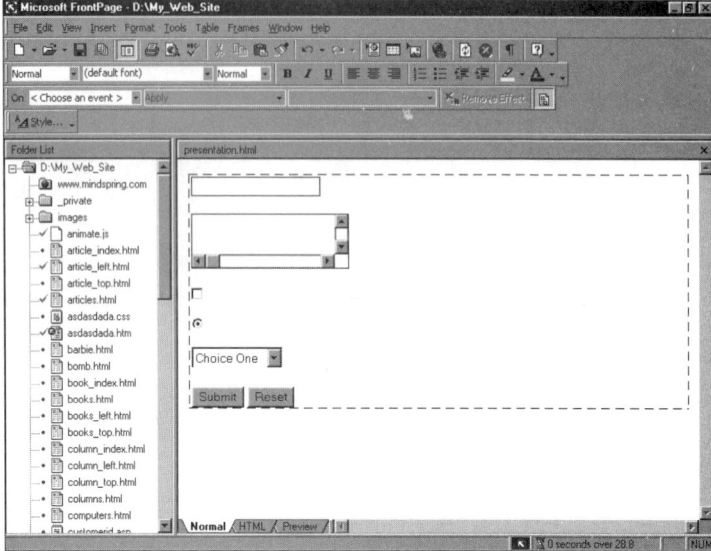

• **Push Button:** Similar to a check box and a radio button, a push button enables users to select a form option simply by clicking the button.

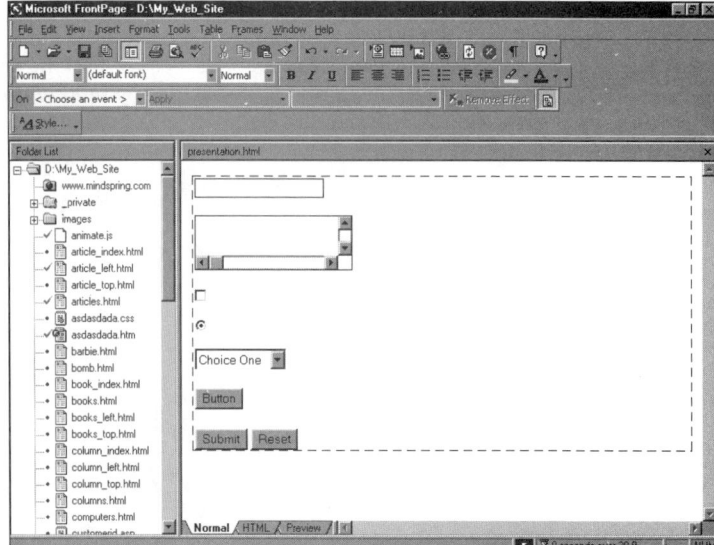

- **Picture:** The picture option lets you specify a .gif image (rather than the standard button) that you use the same way as you would a push button.

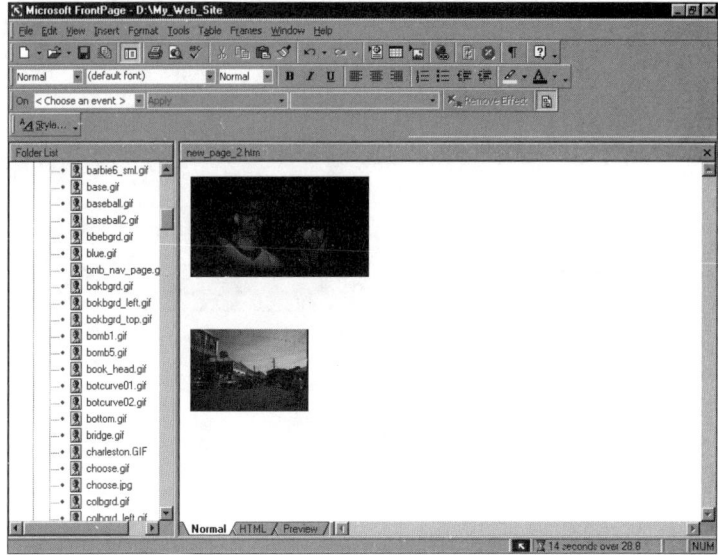

Creating labels for check boxes, radio buttons, push buttons, and pictures

Check boxes, radio buttons, push buttons, and picture buttons inherently don't have any labels associated with them. You, the Web builder, have to create a label for each option that one of these buttons represents. You can't specify more than one label for these kinds of fields because they simply represent either an on or an off state. If you select the option, it's on. If you don't select it, it's off.

The process of adding a label to a button is not the same as adding a value to a button. Labels are just a way of describing the button in the form. You set the value for the button in the button's Property dialog box. *See* the section "Specifying values for form fields," later in this part, for more information about setting field values.

So how do you specify the label for one of these types of buttons? Follow these steps:

1. Insert the button or check box by choosing it from the Insert⇨Form menu.

2. In the Normal View, type the label name (be it text or numeric) for the field, button, or check box where you want it to appear on-screen.

TIP

The label can also be a graphic if, for example, you're choosing from a series of pictures to download.

3. Select both the label text (or graphic) and the check box or button by clicking and dragging over them both.

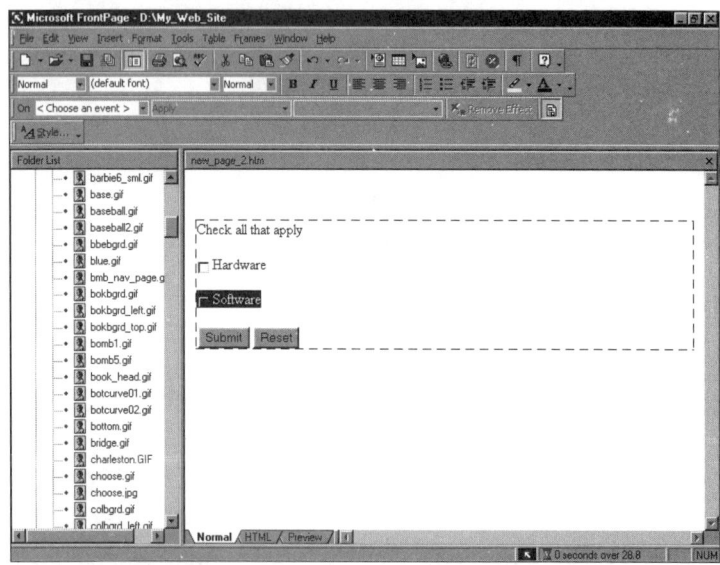

4. Choose Insert⇨Form⇨Label from the menu bar. After you do so, the text or graphic that you selected becomes the label for that button or check box and is passed along when someone submits the form.

Specifying values for form fields

Every form field comes with a default value. Whether it gets sent when the form is submitted is up to the user, but for every field in a form, FrontPage enables you to provide both a name and a default value. In some cases — such as with radio buttons and check boxes — you can also set other properties.

To set the initial values for any form field, double-click the text box, button, or menu in the Normal View. The Properties dialog box for that object appears. You define each text box and menu slightly differently, so the following list highlights how to edit the values for each item.

TIP

One thing that all the properties boxes have in common is the Tab Order field. The number in this field determines the selection order of fields when the user presses the Tab key while filling out the form. This tool is handy when you want a user to, say, fill out the Name text box first and then jump to the Address text box. You'd give the Name text box a Tab Order value of 1 and the Address text box a Tab Order value of 2.

Note: A number of the fields in the form also enable you to restrict the kinds of information provided in a text box, button, or menu. You do this by clicking the Validate button in the field's Property dialog box. You can read more about form Validation in the section "Setting validation for your forms."

+ **One-Line Text Box:** Input the default text into the Initial Value text box in the Text Box Properties dialog box. FrontPage defaults by giving your text boxes utterly unrecognizable names, such as T1. From the Text Box Properties dialog box, you can give your text box a familiar name by typing it in the Name field. Click OK to set the properties for the text box.

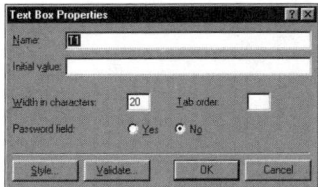

+ **Scrolling Text Box:** As you do for a One-Line Text Box, you input the default text into the Initial Value field in the Scrolling Text Box Properties dialog box. You can also name your field here as you can for a One-Line Text Box. Click OK to set the properties for the text box.

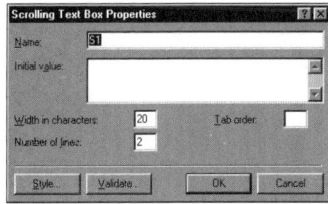

WARNING

Remember: A Scrolling Text Box is designed to have just one default value. Even if you add more than one by pressing Enter and inserting multiple values, users won't be able to select from those extra values. The form treats them all as one value.

✦ **Check Box:** Like those for the One-Line Text Box and the Scrolling Text Box, the Check Box Properties dialog box enables you to specify the name of the check box and the value associated with it in their respective fields. In an additional option called Initial State, by choosing either the Selected or Not Selected radio button, you can set the check box to be either checked or not checked when the form is viewed in a user's Web browser.

✦ **Radio Button:** A radio button works nearly identically to a check box. (See "Setting validation for your forms" later in this part for information about form validation.)

✦ **Drop-Down Menu:** The Drop-Down Menu is the most complex of the form options. From the Drop-Down Menu Properties dialog box, follow these steps to add a value:

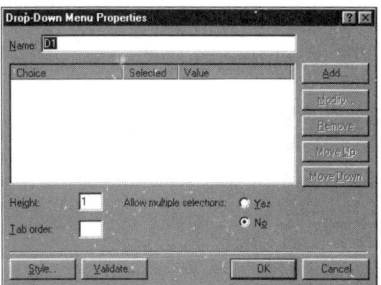

1. Click the Add button to open the Add Choice dialog box, as shown in the following figure.

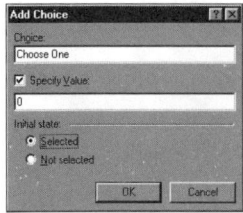

2. Insert a name for the menu in the Choice text box. This text is what the user sees in the drop-down list.

3. Select the Specify Value check box and enter a value in the accompanying text box. This value is sent with the form when a user submits it.

4. Decide whether you want that value to be the default selected value when the user clicks the drop-down menu.

5. Click OK.

6. To add another value, repeat Steps 1 through 5; otherwise, go to Step 7.

7. Back in the Drop-Down Menu Properties dialog box, determine whether you want users to be able to select more than one choice from the drop-down menu by selecting the appropriate Allow Multiple Selections radio button (Yes or No).

8. Click OK to set the values.

✦ **Push Button:** A push button works much like a radio button and a check box, but it, too, has a couple of additional options. One, when you type a name in the Value/label field, the name on the button itself changes. In addition, with a push button, you can set the button type to be a Submit button, a Reset button, or a Normal button.

For a more in-depth analysis of button types in forms and what the various buttons do, check out *HTML For Dummies* by Ed Tittel and Stephen N. James (published by IDG Books Worldwide, Inc.).

✦ **Picture Button:** Strangely enough, your options with a picture button are pretty limited. In fact, unlike the other items, you can't even double-click the picture if you have an Image Editor associated with the graphic type; if you do, it launches the editor instead! To bring up the field properties, you must right-click the image and then choose Field Properties from the pop-up menu. Even then, you can change only one thing: the image's name.

Setting validation for your forms

In many cases, you may find that you want to require users who are filling out forms to fill out a field, select a radio button, or select a particular option. You may also want to restrict the kinds of data they enter in fields — say, only numbers for a telephone field. This process of restricting the number or type of responses a user can input in a form field is called *validation*.

FrontPage 2000 supports validation for text boxes, radio buttons, and drop-down lists. The validation parameters vary from form field to form field, but you access all of them exactly the same way, as follows:

1. In the Normal View, place your cursor where you want to place a form field and then choose <u>I</u>nsert⇨For<u>m</u>⇨*the form field type* from the menu bar.

2. Once the field is in the Web page, double-click the field to bring up the field's property box (for example, if it's a scrolling text box, the Scrolling Text Box Properties dialog box).

3. Click the Validate button to bring up the Validation dialog box. Again, the name of the dialog box is field-specific, although one-line and scrolling text boxes share the same validation parameters.

4. Enter the validation parameters for the field in your form.

The following table lists the basic rules that you can set for each form field type.

Form Field Type	Rules That Can Be Set
One-Line Text Box	Data type (text, integer, or real number), data format (letters, digits, or white space), number format and type (separated by commas or periods), data length (of an entry in characters) and data value constraints (greater or less than a value)
Scrolling Text Box	Data type (text, integer, or real number), data format (letters, digits, or white space), number format and type (separated by commas or periods), data length (of an entry in characters) and data value constraints (greater or less than a value)
Radio Button	Data required (requires that a user choose one of the radio button options in a form if none is selected by default)
Drop-Down Menu	Data required (requires that an item be selected from the form field), disallow first choice (enables you to specify an instruction in the first choice of the menu, such as "Select an Option")

5. Click OK to set the validation parameters and return to the Properties dialog box.

6. Click OK in the Properties dialog box to enable the validation for the form field.

For a more in-depth analysis of button types in forms and what the various buttons do, check out *HTML For Dummies.* For a more in-depth tutorial on using the FrontPage 2000 form validation features, check out *FrontPage 2000 For Dummies.*

Setting form properties

This is perhaps the most important part of building your form. Making sure that the form does exactly what you want it to do involves several steps.

Remember: Before you set your form properties, make sure that you get all your text boxes, boxes, menus, and their corresponding values all set up. (Check out the preceding section for details on how to set up your form values.) You want to have all your data available before you set the properties and start testing your form.

To set your form properties, follow these steps:

1. In the Normal View, select the form for which you want to set the properties by clicking and dragging across that form.

2. Choose Insert⇨Form⇨Form Properties from the menu bar. The Form Properties dialog box appears.

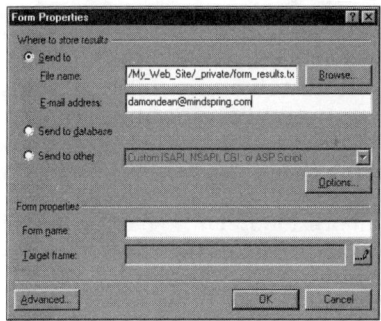

You can also access this screen by right-clicking the form. Then choose Form Properties from the pop-up menu that appears.

3. Choose a location to send your form to after it's posted. FrontPage 2000 supports four different locations for storing the form results:

• **A text file:** This is a simple form of collection, where the form opens a text file, writes the data to the file in comma-separated form, and then saves the file.

• **An e-mail address:** This works much like the text file option except that it sends the data to an e-mail address instead.

• **A database:** If you choose this option and then click OK in the Form Properties dialog box, FrontPage opens another dialog box that prompts you to specify to which database you want the data sent.

See "Adding a Database Connection to a Web" for more information about how to use databases in a Web.

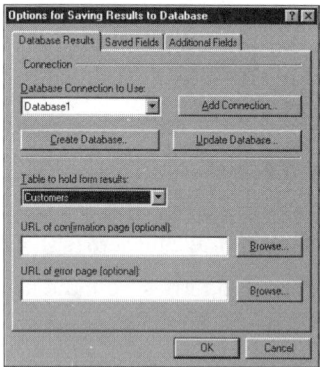

- **Other:** You have several other options for posting data, including posting to an Active Server Page, Discussion Form Handlers, and Registration Form Handlers. For each option, FrontPage 2000 enables you to specify how the form is posted and what the user sees after the posting is complete.

If you want to find out more about how to build forms for things such as databases, registration handlers, and Active Server pages, check out *JavaScript For Dummies*.

Building Pages by Using Style Sheets

Style sheets give you incredible control over your Web pages. If you set the FrontPage compatibility to include the 4.0 browsers, you've probably already used style sheets and didn't even know it. Style sheets are a powerful way to control both the positioning and the look of any object in a Web page. With style sheets, you can

- ✦ Control font properties for individual text elements or apply these properties over a series of pages.

- ✦ Control the exact pixel position of an on-screen object without using a table.

- ✦ Control the layering of objects so that different visual elements can be laid on top of or behind other objects on-screen.

- ✦ Control the visibility of an object.

- ✦ Set page formatting for things such as margins, indents, and paragraphs.

To read the specification for Cascading Style Sheets, check out the Web site for the World Wide Web Consortium at www.w3c.org.

Style sheets are implicit in FrontPage. You never have to see them if you don't want to. At the same time, however, because of the power of this feature, FrontPage 2000 offers you a number of options that give you control over style sheets.

Creating a style sheet

To create a new style sheet, follow these steps:

1. In the Normal View, choose Format⇨Style to open the Style dialog box, as shown in the following figure. From this screen, you can create new styles and edit styles for the standard HTML elements. (*See also* the section "Editing an existing style," later in this part.)

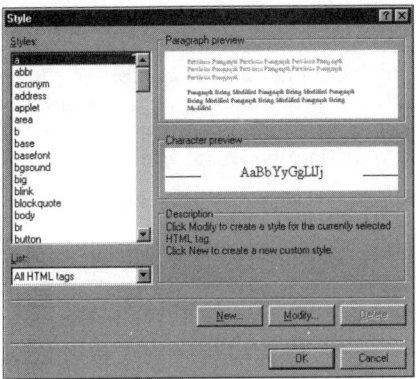

2. Click the New button to open the New Style dialog box.

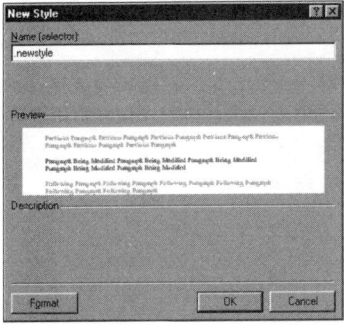

3. Type a name for the style in the Name (selector) text box.

As you name your style, make sure that you begin the name with a period (.) and that there are no spaces in the name. The name **.mystyle** works, but **My Style** doesn't. Unfortunately, FrontPage doesn't warn you about bad style syntax, so if you don't follow this convention, you may never see your style in a page!

4. Click the Format button to reveal the properties that you can edit for that style. For any style, you can specify the following properties. (In each case, the dialog box for that style appears. For example, when you select Font, the Font dialog box comes up. To set the properties for any of the items in your style, be sure to click OK in the dialog box.)

   • **Font:** Sets the typeface, type style, and point size for the style.

     Remember: Although you can set the font properties to be any of the available fonts on your computer, the style won't appear correctly on other users' machines unless they have that font installed on their local systems. As such, it's better to stick to the old standbys: Arial and Times.

   • **Paragraph:** Sets the alignment and indentation for the style.

   • **Border:** Sets the background color, type, and size of borders to the style area, as well as any background patterns.

   • **Numbering:** Sets up bulleted and numbered lists for your style.

   • **Position:** Perhaps the most important option you set, this one affects the on-screen positioning for the style. Unlike in HTML, which assumes that you're always moving from the left side of the screen, with style sheets you can, for example, create an area that's only 300 pixels wide but that starts 200 pixels from the left side of the screen.

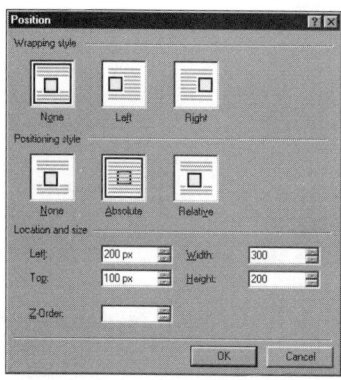

When you choose your positioning, you're best off choosing an <u>A</u>bsolute position, because an absolute position always puts the text exactly where you want it.

When you enter the position, don't bother using the selection buttons for the Le<u>ft</u> and To<u>p</u> fields. FrontPage uses poor syntax on this part of the style sheet. Instead of using 1, 2, 3, 4, and so on, as FrontPage does, use exact pixel locations — reading from left to right and top to bottom on-screen — and include the letters *px* (for *pixels*) at the end of the number. So, for example, a style that starts 200 pixels from the left and 100 pixels down from the top would have the following syntax in the Le<u>ft</u> and To<u>p</u> fields: **200 px**, **100 px**.

5. Click OK in the New Style dialog box to create your new style.

If you want to delete a style, you can do so from the Style dialog box, too. Just select the style that you want to remove from the Styles list and click the Delete button to delete the style.

Editing an existing style

To edit an existing style, follow these steps:

1. In the Normal View, choose F<u>o</u>rmat⇨<u>S</u>tyle to bring up the Style dialog box.

2. In the List box, choose the styles that you want to view. You can choose to edit a style from one of two lists: the All HTML tags list or the User-defined Styles list. You can switch between the two lists by selecting them from the <u>L</u>ist drop-down list.

3. Select the style that you want to modify from the <u>S</u>tyles list.

4. Click the <u>M</u>odify button to access the Modify Style dialog box.

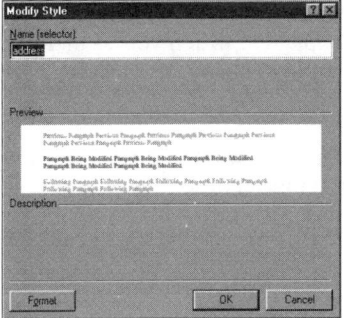

5. Modify the style the same way that you create a new style, as I described earlier in "Creating a Style Sheet."

6. Click OK to save your changes to the style.

FrontPage 2000 doesn't have a Reset to Defaults option for styles, so be careful editing the base HTML styles. You may want to write down the presets before going in and editing them too heavily.

Applying a style

Applying a style in FrontPage 2000 is just like applying a style in Word. To apply a style, perform the following steps:

1. Highlight the text to which you want to apply a style.

2. Click the arrow of the Style selection drop-down list box.

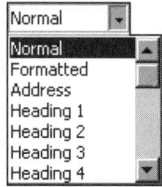

3. Scroll down the list and select the style you want.

Looking at the Style list is also a good way to double-check that a style that you've created is working correctly. All user-defined styles that begin with a period appear at the bottom of the Style list.

Applying styles to more than one page

If you're building a Web site with a lot of pages and you want to apply a variety of styles across those pages, FrontPage provides an easy way to accomplish this task. For this method to work, however, you must have a page in which you've included all the styles that you want to employ on a series of Web pages.

Here's how to apply styles to more than one page:

1. Create an empty HTML page with all the styles that you want to include across a number of other pages.

See also "Creating Web Pages" in Part II.

2. Choose File⇨Save As to open the Save As dialog box. Select Hypertext Style Sheet (.css) from the Save As drop-down list. Name the style and then click OK to save the style.

3. Select the Folders View by clicking Folders in the Views window.

4. Select the pages to which you want to apply the multitude of styles by holding down the Ctrl key and clicking each file you want to apply the style to.

5. Choose Format⇨Style Sheet Links from the menu bar to open the Link Style Sheet dialog box, as shown in the following figure.

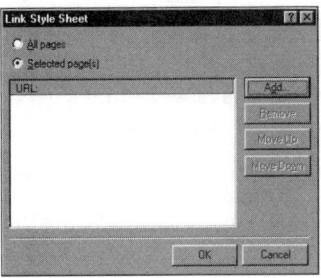

6. Click the Add button.

7. From the Select Hyperlink dialog box that appears, choose the Hyperlink Style Sheet (.css) file that you just created and then click OK.

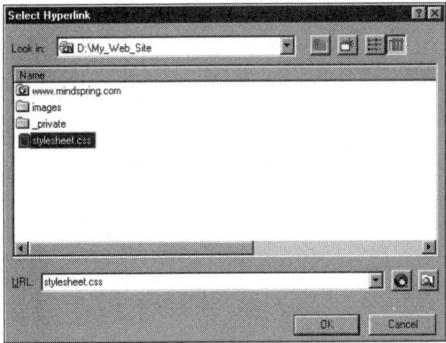

8. In the Links Style Sheet dialog box that appears, click OK to link the style sheet to the selected pages.

To double-check that everything is working properly, take a peek at the Style list on the Formatting Toolbar. The styles that you're including in the Hypertext Style Sheet page should appear at the bottom of the available styles list.

Creating Dynamic HTML Effects

Dynamic HTML is both exactly what it sounds like and a complete misnomer at the same time — and, frankly, that's a pretty tough combination to pull off. On the one hand, Dynamic HTML uses HTML 3.2 or above to house the functions that make a whole bunch of cool stuff happen. On the other hand, the real underpinnings of Dynamic HTML lie in the JavaScript that's needed to make it work correctly and in a variety of Web browsers.

In this case, "a variety of Web browsers" means Netscape Navigator 4.0 or higher and Internet Explorer 4.0 or higher. Older browsers don't support the *Document Object Model* (DOM) syntax that Dynamic HTML employs.

So what's the bottom line? Quite simply, Dynamic HTML enables Web builders to

✦ Animate text and graphics.

✦ Produce cool visual effects.

✦ Move objects around on-screen.

✦ Change text colors and styles.

Dynamic HTML is a good way to spice up an otherwise dull Web page, but you have to be careful. As cool as it is, Dynamic HTML has some inherent limitations:

✦ It's a processor hog that can really bring your system to a crawl if you're trying to animate too many things on the page at the same time.

✦ It limits the interactivity mostly to rollovers, mouse clicks, and page loads.

✦ Compatibility is an issue because Netscape and Microsoft are still using different versions of the Document Object Model (which is the underlying syntax that controls the behaviors of objects on-screen).

Before you can apply any of the Dynamic HTML effects in FrontPage 2000, you must activate the Dynamic HTML toolbar. To do so, choose Format⇨Dynamic HTML Effects from the menu bar. This action activates the toolbar and places it just below the Formatting Toolbar on-screen.

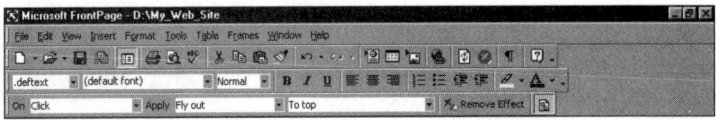

All the Dynamic HTML events in FrontPage fall into the same basic structure:

1. Choose the event that triggers the effect, such as a mouse click.

2. Choose the effect, such as an animation.

3. Specify the effect, such as moving the graphic left to right.

Creating text rollovers

A text rollover is the process of changing a snippet of text when a user runs the mouse cursor over that piece of text. You can use this effect as a tool to highlight the text, or even use it as a hyperlink. To create a text rollover in FrontPage 2000, follow these steps:

1. In the Normal View, type the text that you want to act as a rollover.

2. Highlight the text to which you want the effect to apply when the mouse cursor rolls over it.

3. From the Dynamic HTML Toolbar, select Mouse Over from the On drop-down list.

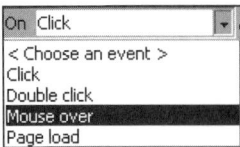

4. From the Apply drop-down list, choose Formatting. Notice that Formatting is the only option available in a text-based mouse-over event. *Remember:* For every event, you can choose among different effects. The same is true for specifying an effect. The formatting of the effect changes depending on the exact effect.

5. Select Choose Font from the third drop-down list. The Font dialog box appears.

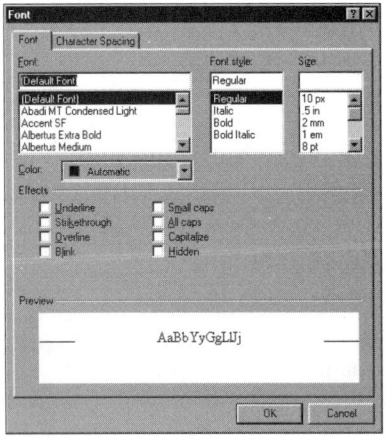

6. From the Color list, choose a new color for the text.

7. Click OK to set the rollover color.

You can change a number of the other text properties in the Font dialog box as well, including the point size, the font style, and even the font type. You can also change the character settings by selecting the Character Spacing tab.

Moving text and graphics off-screen

FrontPage 2000 is pretty limited in the number of ways in which it enables you to move objects around on-screen. By and large, all you can do is have them start on-screen and then move someplace. That said, FrontPage makes moving objects *off* the screen a snap. Here's how to do so:

1. In the Normal View, insert the graphic or type the text that you want to move around on-screen.

See Part IV for more information about inserting text and graphics into a Web page.

2. Select the graphic or highlight the text.

3. Select an event from the On list of the Dynamic HTML Toolbar to choose your event start.

4. From the Apply list, select Fly Out.

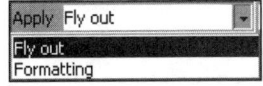

5. From the options in the list to the right of the Apply list, choose the way in which you want the graphic or text to leave the screen. The formatting is automatically applied to the object.

Inserting Java Applets

FrontPage uses Java for a lot of the special effects that you see on-screen, such as page transitions. Most of the Java that controls these effects is transparent to the user . . . unless, of course, you happen to take a peek at the HTML. If you have an applet of your own that you want to embed in your Web page, FrontPage provides a clean little interface for doing just that. Here's how:

1. Choose Insert➪Advanced➪Java Applet to bring up the Java Applet Properties dialog box, as shown in the following figure.

2. Insert the name of the Java applet code in the Applet Source text box. (Usually, applet code comes with a .class file extension.)

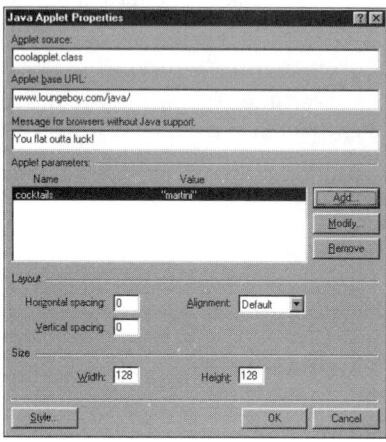

3. Insert the URL location of the code in the Applet Base URL text box.

4. For browsers that don't support Java, include a message telling users that this page contains an applet. Insert that message in the Message for Browsers without Java Support text box.

5. Add any parameter values to that area of the dialog box. Most Java applets come with a series of variables that you can specify. All these variables share the same syntax. Click the Add button to access the Set Attribute Value dialog box. Give the parameter a name by typing it in the Name field and a value by typing it in the Value field. Then click OK to set the parameter.

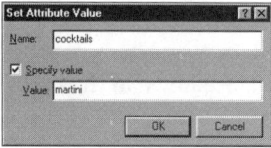

6. Set the Layout, Size, and Style options for the applet in the appropriate areas of the Java Applet Properties dialog box. These are the same options that you'd set for any object on a Web page, including such things as position, alignment, and font.

See "Building Pages by Using Style Sheets" earlier in this part, as well as Part IV, for more information about inserting text and graphics into a Web page.

7. Click OK to insert the applet into your Web page.

A good place to get some basic information about using Java and get some beginning Java applets is www.developer.com.

Want to find out more about Java? Pick up a copy of *Java For Dummies,* 3rd Edition, by Aaron E. Walsh (published by IDG Books Worldwide, Inc.).

Inserting Plug-ins

The FrontPage 2000 interface for adding plug-ins for things such as Flash, RealAudio, and QuickTime essentially mirrors that for adding Java applets. FrontPage assumes nothing about the plug-in itself, nor does it automate the process of embedding the plug-in. In other words, you're pretty much on your own.

To insert a plug-in object, follow these steps:

1. In the Normal View, choose Insert⇨Advanced⇨Plug-in to open the Plug-In Properties dialog box.

2. In the Data Source text box, type the path to the source file for the plug-in. You can also click the Browse button to search through your Web, the available local/network drives, or the Internet for the data source.

3. In the Message for Browsers without Plug-in Support text box, type a message for users whose browsers don't support the plug-in. A sample message might read something like, "You don't have Macromedia's Flash player. To download it, please visit www.macromedia.com."

4. Set the layout, size, and style options for the applet by clicking the Style Button. Doing so brings up the Modify Style dialog box. These are the same options that you'd set for any object on a Web page, including position, alignment, and font.

See "Building Pages by Using Style Sheets" in this part, as well as Part IV, for more information about inserting text and graphics into a Web page.

5. Click OK to insert the plug-in in your Web page.

My experience with FrontPage and plug-ins is that you're generally better off inserting plug-ins by hand. You have greater flexibility over the HTML, which is often necessary if you're checking for things such as browser types and whether a plug-in is installed on a user's browser. For most plug-ins, the manufacturer (for example, Macromedia with Flash) provides useful tips and, in many cases, the proper HTML to enable and/or download the plug-in.

Techie Talk

ActiveX: The Microsoft Windows technology that enables Web developers to access Windows programs and utilities through their Web browsers.

add-in: A program developed either by Microsoft or by another third party that adds functionality to a copy of FrontPage 2000.

applet: A mini-program that you can use to make FrontPage even more powerful, such as Microsoft Help and Visual Basic Editor.

Auto Thumbnail: A handy tool that enables you to create a mini-version of a picture.

banner: A set of similarly sized images, usually either at the top or the bottom of a Web page, that a user scrolls through when arriving on a Web page. Banners are commonly used as a method of promoting advertising messages, as well as key pieces of information that you want users to know.

beveling: Adds both a border and three-dimensional depth to a graphic.

brightness: The lightness or darkness of a graphic.

comment: A Web element that lets you make notes about how you might change things in the future or just reminds you of how or why you did something in your HTML. Although comments are embedded in the source of the Web page, they are not visible to viewers of the page through a Web browser.

component: A cool FrontPage feature that doesn't seem to fit anywhere else. Components include Office elements such as Excel spreadsheets, Web elements such as banners and hit counters, page composition tools, and property management tools.

contrast: How much a graphic's individual pixels stand out.

cookie: A small snippet of text that's added to your computer by a Web browser. Usually, this text includes some information about you, such as your e-mail address or your name. The cookie can then be retrieved the next time you visit the site that added it.

crop: To cut an image down in size.

frame: The process of splitting one Web page into a series of Web pages all displayed together within the browser window at the same time.

FTP (File Transfer Protocol): The process by which files are transferred from your computer to a server on the Internet.

GIF image: The file format of a graphic that is viewable in a Web browser over the Internet.

hit counter: A Web element that tracks the number of times a page has been accessed and displays that number on the Web page itself.

hover button: A button that animates or highlights when you roll your mouse cursor over it.

HTML (HyperText Markup Language): The language of the Internet, used to build Web pages.

HTML editor: A product that creates Web pages by using HTML.

hyperlink: A way of jumping from location to location within a series of Web pages. Hyperlinks are the navigational building blocks of any Web site.

hyperlink status: In FrontPage, the state of a hyperlink at any given time. If a hyperlink is not functioning, the hyperlink status is said to be broken.

image editor: A tool used to create and manipulate graphics files.

image map: A great navigation tool that you see in many Web sites. You load a Web page, and there's a big graphic smack dab in the middle of the page. On the graphic are a host of different links to various locations.

load time: The time it takes, on average, to load a Web page, given the speed of the modem used to load it.

macro: Essentially, a set of automated tasks that FrontPage does for you.

marquee: A block of text that moves across the screen, as in a stock ticker.

navigation bar: A series of hyperlinks on a Web page that help you navigate through the structure of the site.

Navigation View: Provides a visual representation of all the pages on your site and how they're ordered hierarchically. By dragging around the pages, you can change the relationships of those pages to one another and organize the pages of your site more effectively.

Normal Mode: FrontPage's visual editor for Web development. Users can place elements — text, graphics, applets, whatever — on-screen in any location, and HTML is generated automatically to account for the location of every object on-screen.

OLE (object linking and embedding): The common Microsoft program language that enables developers to build programs, applets, and scripts that can be used across all Microsoft Office applications.

page banner: A quick and easy way to add a title to a Web page.

Page View: Where you build all your Web pages. From this view, you can create Web pages, view the HTML source for those pages, and even preview the pages in a browser-like window.

parameters: Let you specify a variable for your Web project and then call it in the FrontPage Editor while you're building pages.

pixel: A dot that represents a point on-screen. In a 640 x 480 screen size, for example, there are 640 pixels from the left to right sides of the screen and 480 pixels from top to bottom.

pixel precise positioning: The capability to place an object — say, a graphic or some text — at a precise location on-screen.

Preview Mode: Lets you see just what your pages are going to look like in a Web browser window before you put them up on the Internet. The default browser for FrontPage 2000 is Internet Explorer.

report: In FrontPage 2000, information that the program provides about various elements of your Web.

Reports View: Here, you get an immediate Site Summary, which gives you a bird's-eye view of what's working (or not working, as the case may be) within your Web site. From this view, you also can run a more detailed series of reports that give you immediate information about the status of various aspects of your Web site, such as load times or hyperlink status.

RGB: A color-matching scheme based on mixing and matching red, green, and blue color values to represent more than 16 million unique colors.

scale: To make an entire image either larger or smaller.

shared border: A feature that lets you designate a region of a Web page as shared and then apply changes to that region on just one page. Automatically, FrontPage makes the change across every other page with the same Shared Border.

source control: The management of files across multiple users, including who works on a file, when that person works on it, and what privileges the person has while working on it.

task: Basically, a fancy-looking to-do list.

Tasks View: A FrontPage view in which you can assign tasks to individuals on your team, check the status of tasks underway, and manage the workflow and publishing of new elements to the site.

template: A standardized version of a Web page that includes a number of common elements already built into the page. Templates generally include standardized type styles, graphics, and even page layouts.

text rollover: A piece of text that changes its size, color, or font properties by virtue of someone moving the mouse cursor over the top of it.

theme: A common look and feel for an entire Web provided by common graphical styles, as well the same text and layout styles across all the pages in that Web.

transitions: Include things like wipes, fades, and reveals. They're designed to add a dramatic flavor to an otherwise boring Web link interaction.

view: In FrontPage, one of the six different ways to look at a Web or Web page. The six views are Normal, Folders, Hyperlink, Navigation, Reports, and Task.

Views Bar: The really big menu with all the icons that runs down the left-hand side of the screen. It's the easiest way to access the vast majority of features that make up FrontPage 2000.

Web: An entire Web site. Also known as a Web project.

Web page: An HTML page within a Web.

z-index: In Cascading Style Sheets, the positioning order of a layered object. Objects with a higher z-index value are on top of those layered objects with a lower z-index value.

Index

Dummies Books™
Bestsellers on Every Topic!

Discover Dummies™ Online!

The *Dummies* Web Site is your fun and friendly online resource for the latest information about *...For Dummies*® books on all your favorite topics. From cars to computers, wine to Windows, and investing to the Internet, we've got a shelf full of *...For Dummies* books waiting for you!

Ten Fun and Useful Things You Can Do at www.dummies.com

1. Register this book and win!
2. Find and buy the *...For Dummies* books you want online.
3. Get ten great *Dummies Tips*™ every week.
4. Chat with your favorite *...For Dummies* authors.
5. Subscribe free to *The Dummies Dispatch*™ newsletter.
6. Enter our sweepstakes and win cool stuff.
7. Send a free cartoon postcard to a friend.
8. Download free software.
9. Sample a book before you buy.
10. Talk to us. Make comments, ask questions, and get answers!

Jump online to these ten fun and useful things at
http://www.dummies.com/10useful

For other technology titles from IDG Books Worldwide, go to
www.idgbooks.com

Not online yet? It's easy to get started with *The Internet For Dummies*® 5th Edition, or *Dummies 101*®: *The Internet For Windows*® 98, available at local retailers everywhere.

Find other *...For Dummies* books on these topics:
Business • Careers • Databases • Food & Beverages • Games • Gardening • Graphics
Hardware • Health & Fitness • Internet and the World Wide Web • Networking • Office Suites
Operating Systems • Personal Finance • Pets • Programming • Recreation • Sports
Spreadsheets • Teacher Resources • Test Prep • Word Processing

IDG BOOKS WORLDWIDE BOOK REGISTRATION

Register This Book and Win!

We want to hear from you!

Visit **http://my2cents.dummies.com** to register this book and tell us how you liked it!

- ✔ Get entered in our monthly prize giveaway.

- ✔ Give us feedback about this book — tell us what you like best, what you like least, or maybe what you'd like to ask the author and us to change!

- ✔ Let us know any other *...For Dummies*® topics that interest you.

Your feedback helps us determine what books to publish, tells us what coverage to add as we revise our books, and lets us know whether we're meeting your needs as a *...For Dummies* reader. You're our most valuable resource, and what you have to say is important to us!

Not on the Web yet? It's easy to get started with *Dummies 101*®: *The Internet For Windows*® *98* or *The Internet For Dummies*, 5th Edition, at local retailers everywhere.

Or let us know what you think by sending us a letter at the following address:

...For Dummies Book Registration
Dummies Press
7260 Shadeland Station, Suite 100
Indianapolis, IN 46256-3945
Fax 317-596-5498

BESTSELLING
BOOK SERIES